RIVERS IN AMERICAN LIFE AND TIMES

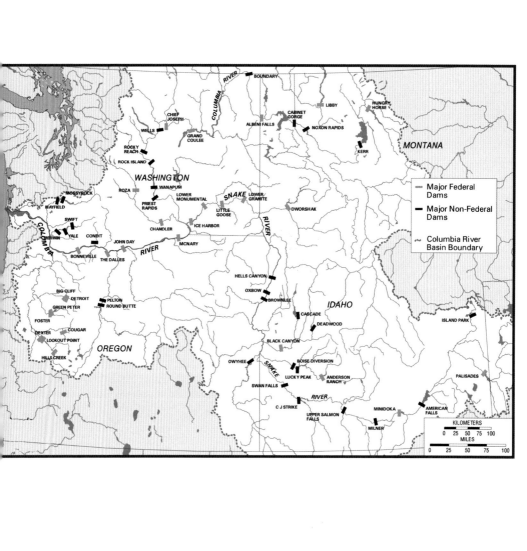

BOUNDARY

COLUMBIA RIVER

LIBBY
HUNGRY HORSE

CHIEF JOSEPH
WELLS
GRAND COULEE
ROCKY REACH
ROCK ISLAND

CABINET GORGE
ALBENI FALLS
NOXON RAPIDS

MONTANA

KERR

WASHINGTON

ROZA
WANAPUM
PRIEST RAPIDS
LOWER MONUMENTAL
SNAKE
LOWER GRANITE

MOSSYROCK
MAYFIELD
SWIFT
YALE
MERWIN
CONDIT
COLUMBIA
CHANDLER
JOHN DAY
RIVER
BONNEVILLE
THE DALLES
LITTLE GOOSE
ICE HARBOR
MCNARY
RIVER
DWORSHAK

SNAKE

HELLS CANYON
OXBOW
BROWNLEE

BIG CLIFF
DETROIT
GREEN PETER
PELTON
ROUND BUTTE
FOSTER
COUGAR
DEXTER
LOOKOUT POINT
HILLS CREEK

OREGON

CASCADE
DEADWOOD

IDAHO

ISLAND PARK

BLACK CANYON

OWYHEE
SNAKE
BOISE DIVERSION
LUCKY PEAK
ANDERSON RANCH
SWAN FALLS
RIVER
PALISADES

C J STRIKE
UPPER SALMON FALLS
MINIDOKA
AMERICAN FALLS
MILNER

	Major Federal Dams
	Major Non-Federal Dams
~	Columbia River Basin Boundary

KILOMETERS
0 25 50 75 100
MILES
0 25 50 75 100

THE
COLUMBIA
RIVER

Tom Lashnits

CHELSEA HOUSE
PUBLISHERS
A Haights Cross Communications Company

Philadelphia

FRONTIS: The Columbia River flows across almost 1,250 miles of mountains, desert, and coastal plain to its mouth at the Pacific Ocean. This map shows the boundary of what is considered to be the Columbia River Basin and shows both the major federal and non-federal dams that have been built since the Rock Island Dam was built in 1933.

CHELSEA HOUSE PUBLISHERS

VP, NEW PRODUCT DEVELOPMENT Sally Cheney
DIRECTOR OF PRODUCTION Kim Shinners
CREATIVE MANAGER Takeshi Takahashi
MANUFACTURING MANAGER Diann Grasse

Staff for THE COLUMBIA RIVER

EXECUTIVE EDITOR Lee Marcott
PRODUCTION EDITOR Megan Emery
PHOTO EDITOR Sarah Bloom
SERIES AND COVER DESIGNER Keith Trego
LAYOUT 21st Century Publishing and Communications, Inc.

A Haights Cross Communications Company

www.chelseahouse.com

First Printing

9 8 7 6 5 4 3 2 1

Library of Congress Cataloging-in-Publication Data applied for.

ISBN 0-7910-7728-4 HC   0-7910-8003-X PB

T 102016

CONTENTS

1

Promise of a River

The Columbia River flows across almost 1,250 miles of mountains, desert, and coastal plain, from its source high in the mountains of British Columbia to its mouth at the Pacific Ocean. This river offers the only passageway to the interior of North America from the Pacific—the single route that cuts through the coastal mountains and opens the way to the Rockies.

The Columbia was therefore destined to become a primary route for early nineteenth-century traders and settlers traveling in and out of Oregon territory, which eventually became the states of Oregon, Washington, and Idaho. The river developed as a major thoroughfare not because it provided an easy waterway for ships and boats to navigate—the river was far too rough and wild for that—but because it was the only passable river for thousands of miles.

As a major geographic marker, the Columbia was later chosen to delineate the boundary between Oregon and Washington. Its major tributary, the Snake River, now forms part of the boundary between Oregon and Idaho. Even today, freighters travel as far inland as Portland, 100 miles from the Pacific Ocean, and sea-going barges are towed as far as Lewiston, Idaho, another 360 miles upstream, making Lewiston the farthest inland seaport in North America.

The river begins as glacial drip in the Canadian Rockies. A number of rivulets come together to form Columbia Lake, which is sandwiched between the Rocky Mountains on the east and the Selkirk Range to the west. Columbia Lake is 2,650 feet above sea level. That's more than half a mile high. When water rushes down that much slope in 1,250 miles, it makes a fast and powerful river. The Columbia drops almost twice the height of the Mississippi in about half the distance.

The Columbia is not only wild, it's also remote. It was discovered much later than other American rivers, and it developed later as well. While stately homes were being built along the Hudson and riverboats paddled up and down the

The Columbia River surges from the mountains of British Columbia 1,250 miles to its mouth at the Pacific Ocean, shown here. The river and its tributaries carry over one-fifth of the fresh water running out of North America. That's more water than any other river that flows from North or South America into the Pacific. In all, the Columbia drains an area the size of Texas.

Mississippi, fur trappers, missionaries, and settlers were still battling the elements in the Northwest. As late as 1870, only about 800 whites lived north of Walla Walla in the great expanses of eastern Washington. Even today, there is only one major city on the Columbia: Portland, Oregon.

In an unusual configuration, Columbia Lake, at the river's source, sits only a mile away from one of the Columbia's major tributaries, the Kootenay River. The Kootenay originates in the

Canadian Rockies, to the northeast of the Columbia, and flows south right past Columbia Lake, separated from it only by a low mountain pass called Canal Flats.

The Columbia itself heads in the opposite direction, twisting north between two high mountain ranges for about 200 miles. Then the Columbia turns sharply to the west, makes a U-turn around the Selkirk Range, and heads south, pushing for the United States. For these first few hundred miles, the Columbia courses through wild, unbroken mountains and forests—still relatively undeveloped in the twenty-first century—and then flows through an inland sea called Arrow Lake, a 130-mile-long body of water set amid the mountains, before crossing the U.S. border.

Meanwhile, the Kootenay, after it passes the Columbia, dips south into Montana and Idaho, where the American spelling of its name is "Kootenai." Then this tributary swings back north to meet the Columbia above the Canadian border. After passing within a mile of the Columbia, the Kootenay traverses almost 600 miles first to the south and then north, and the Columbia travels more than 400 miles, first pushing to the north then heading south.

The Columbia River then joins forces with another tributary, the Pend Oreille, and powers its way across the international boundary into Washington State. About 40 miles below the border lay Kettle Falls, where Native Americans once congregated to fish for salmon. The falls dropped a total of 25 feet in two levels. They are no longer visible; they were drowned under Franklin D. Roosevelt Lake after Grand Coulee Dam was built in the 1930s.

When the river flows out of Canada and into eastern Washington, it leaves behind the pine-covered mountains of British Columbia and enters a drier climate of rolling hills and gouged-out valleys. As the Spokane River meets the Columbia, the river makes a big bend to the west, circling around a giant plateau of hard basalt that was deposited by volcanic activity in ancient times. For several hundred miles, the Columbia arches around the Columbia Basin, meandering south through eastern Washington.

Most of this region was once a dry wasteland. Now much of it has been turned into rich farmland by irrigation from the river. Though the land is now bountiful, the climate is still dry—hot in the summer and cold in the winter.

After the Columbia joins forces with the Snake River, it turns west again to form the border between Washington and Oregon, carving through a ridge of hills in a depression called the Wallula Gap. Then the great Columbia gathers itself for the assault on the Cascade Mountains. Lewis and Clark named the mountain range the Cascades after coming upon a magnificent waterfall at the Great Gorge of the Columbia, now also flooded by the dams. The two American explorers referred to the surrounding mountains as "the mountains by the Cascades," eventually shortened to "the Cascades."

As the river cuts through the mountains, the climate turns more temperate and the river is cloaked in fog and rain. The river originally sliced through the mountains in a tumble of rapids and swirling currents as it carved an 85-mile-long route through the hard young rock. This once posed a dangerous obstacle to the canoes of the Native Americans and the boats of early fur traders. Some of the first Oregon settlers tried to raft these waters, usually with disastrous results, but most chose to carry their conveyances around the most dangerous waters at Celilo Falls, The Dalles, and the Cascades. All of these rapids and swirling eddies are now covered by long, placid lakes.

By the time the river flows out of the Cascades, it is almost at sea level. The river broadens, and the effects of ocean tides can be felt. The Willamette River, the last major tributary to the Columbia, enters from the south at the city of Portland, 100 miles from the ocean. Beyond Portland, the river widens and is dotted with islands, but there is no soft, squishy Mississippi-like delta at the mouth of the Columbia. Instead, the huge volume of fresh water pushes straight over the sandbars and into the sea.

THE EARTH IS STILL ALIVE

Like all the Cascades, Mount St. Helens is a product of the collision of the ocean plates with the continental plates, which forces magma and steam to the surface of the earth. This activity, which formed Mount Rainier, the tallest of the Cascades, a million years ago, is still going on. On May 18, 1980, that fact was starkly realized.

At 8:32 A.M., an earthquake registering 5.1 on the Richter scale shook the landscape, rattling windows and waking people throughout southern Washington. Then the north side of Mount St. Helens exploded with a force several hundred times the power of the atomic bomb dropped on Hiroshima. The heat from the blast reached 680°F. The heat, ash, and debris exploding from the volcano killed 57 people that day. The rock, snow, and ice that blasted from the north face slid down the mountain in an avalanche that thundered at up to 200 mph.

This collapse along the side of the mountain flooded Spirit Lake and formed a mile-wide dam of rocks and trees and other debris, blocking Toutle River. When the dam overflowed, a maelstrom surged down the mountain, washing out bridges, sweeping away houses, and flushing away trees and fallen timber. The flood tumbled down the Toutle into the Cowlitz and then into the Columbia. About 22 million cubic feet of silt washed into the Columbia River, forming mud banks and filling up the channel.

Another blast followed the avalanche, sending pulverized pieces of rock and other materials flying into the atmosphere at 400 mph. Trees and animals were killed within a 150-square-mile area. The Washington State Department of Game estimated that 4 billion board-feet of timber were destroyed—that's enough wood to build 300,000 two-bedroom homes. Also, nearly 7,000 large animals—deer, elk, and bear—were killed by the eruption, along with most of the birds and small mammals living on the face of the mountain and an estimated 12 million young salmon trapped in nearby hatcheries.

Meanwhile, ash rose to a height of 90,000 feet, darkening the skies east into Montana and eventually circling the globe. In eastern Washington, the ash accumulated several inches deep and the sky was so dark the streetlights came on. In all, 540 million tons of material rained down on the Northwest. When all was said and done, more than 1,300 feet had been blown off the top of the mountain.

Could it happen again? Mount St. Helens is an active volcano. It's possible we will see another powerful eruption in our lifetimes.

Theodore Winthrop, who traveled the Columbia River environs in 1853, described the scene:

> A wall of terrible breakers marks the mouth of the Columbia,
> Achilles of rivers. Other mighty streams may swim feebly
> away seaward, may sink into foul marshes, may trickle
> through ditches of an oozy delta, may scatter among sandbars
> the currents that once moved majestic and united. But to this
> heroic flood was destined a short life and a glorious one—a
> life all one strong, victorious struggle, from the mountains to
> the sea.[1]

The Columbia empties more water into the Pacific than does any other river in North or South America. One-fifth of the fresh water running out of North America comes down the Columbia River. In all, the Columbia system drains 250,000 square miles—everything west of the Continental Divide from southern British Columbia to parts of Montana, Wyoming, Utah, Nevada, as well as most of Idaho, Oregon, and Washington. The river and its 150 tributaries drain an area about the size of Texas. It carries twice the amount of water as the Missouri and nearly ten times the water of the Colorado.

Its major tributaries are the Kootenay, which flows mostly in Canada but dips into Montana before meeting the Columbia just north of the Canadian border, and the Pend Oreille, the Spokane, the Okanogan, the Wenatchee, the Yakima, the Walla Walla, the Umatilla, the Deschutes, the Willamette, and the Cowlitz. The Snake River is the Columbia's largest tributary. It is only 200 miles shorter than the Columbia itself, and it collects waters from the Salmon River, the Clearwater River, and a showering of others.

Before the modern dams were built—the first was Rock Island Dam, completed in 1933, and the last was Canada's Revelstoke Dam, finished in 1984—Chinook salmon swam as far inland as the Continental Divide, nosing their way deep into Idaho, Montana, and British Columbia. The major tributaries

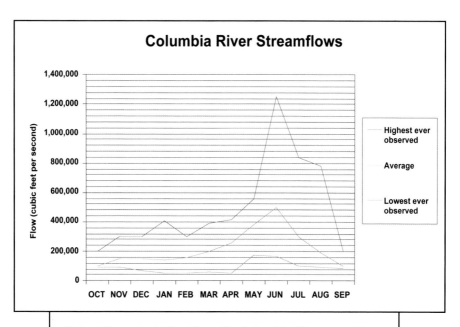

Columbia River Streamflows

Before the arrival of settlers, the Columbia River was wild and powerful, hurtling down from its origin at Columbia Lake, 2,650 miles above sea level, to the Pacific Ocean. During its period of peak flow in late spring, the water rushed through the wilderness at over 1,000,000 cubic feet per second. Historic records show an annual pattern with peak flows in the spring. [Source: U.S. Bureau of Reclamation, U.S. Army Corps of Engineers, and Bonneville Power Administration. *The Columbia River System: The Inside Story*, Portland OR, 1991, p.6]

of the Columbia provided highways for fish to cross the desert east of the Cascades until they climbed up into their mountain spawning places. Then the natural life cycle of the salmon caused them to die in the streambeds, leaving their progeny to make the trip back to the sea, eventually to return to the mountains, where another generation was conceived and born.

Today there are 14 major dams blocking the Columbia River, backing up lakes behind each one. The Mica Dam, in Canada, is the first and the highest on the river. The great

Grand Coulee Dam is by far the largest. The Bonneville Dam, just above Portland, sits closest to the river's mouth. There are another 130 dams along the Columbia's tributaries, all designed to back up the river, provide deep water navigation for boats and barges, distribute water to farmers tilling the arid land, and generate electricity for the millions of people who now live in the Columbia region.

It wasn't always that way. When the pioneers found the Columbia, and for 150 years after that, the river raged unchecked through deep gorges, bubbled past dangerous rapids, and tumbled over powerful falls, all in a race to get to the Pacific. Even though it has now been harnessed for energy and irrigation, the Columbia is still a young, restless, powerful body of water. It can suck an entire tree into one of its whirlpools, then spit the tree 20 feet into the air before it plunges back into the churning water.

What gave rise to this powerful river and the rough, raw land that surrounds it? Millions of years ago, the Blue Mountains, now in eastern Oregon, were a headland, with the Pacific Ocean splashing up against their shores. Much of the area of what is now Oregon and Washington lay underwater, which explains how fossils have been found high up in the Cascade Mountains of western Washington. One spot on Mount Baker has so many shell fossils that it is called Chowder Ridge.

Then volcanoes began to pour out lava in as many as 200 separate eruptions over thousands of years. The ocean floor buckled, forming a chain of islands to the west. Volcanic material swept down the mountain slopes and spread out over 80,000 square miles of what is now western Idaho and eastern Washington and Oregon.

First, this lava raised the land, giving rise to the Columbia Plateau. The volcanic outflow also shoved the ancient Columbia River to the north and west, forming what is now the big bend of the Columbia. Weighed down by all the basalt, the earth's crust gradually sank, leaving a basin that is 2,000 to 4,000 feet above sea level at its edges but only 500 feet above sea level at its lowest point. The area, today called the Columbia Basin, is composed of volcanic rock, which in some places is as much as two miles thick, overlaying fragments of the earth's original crust.

As the Cascades rose, they formed the prominent peaks that can be seen today. In Washington, they are Mount Baker, Mount Rainier, Mount Adams, and Mount St. Helens, and in Oregon, they are Mount Hood, the Three Sisters, and Mt. Mazama to the south, which has Crater Lake nestled in its peak. The ever-flowing Columbia cut a V-shaped canyon through the rising land, allowing the river to reach the Pacific.

During the Ice Age, from 2 million to 12,000 years ago, the Cascades were carved by the ebb and flow of the ice. The craggy peaks and U-shaped valleys were formed by glaciers advancing in waves from the north and then retreating during warmer periods. To the northwest, Puget Sound was once under an ice sheet 4,000 feet thick. Only after the ice melted was the sound unveiled.

The Ice Age came in four stages, each lasting tens of thousands of years. Every time the ice retreated it brought glacial floods, raising the level of the sea and depositing rocks and sediments across the land. The silt left behind by the glaciers eroded into dust and was blown around by prehistoric winds. It settled across the Northwest, up to 150 feet thick in some places. These glacial deposits now form the fertile farmland that makes the Columbia Plateau one of the great food-producing areas of the world.

The last Ice Age began 70,000 years ago. So much water was frozen in the glaciers that sea level was perhaps 300 feet lower than it is today, exposing a broad coastal plain along the shoreline of what is today Oregon and Washington. The climate around the Columbia was like Alaska is today. Herds of great mammals—mammoths, bison, caribou, and prehistoric horses and camels—ranged over the land. Evidence suggests that there were also humans living around the Columbia, descendants of primitive people who trekked across the

Bering land bridge from Asia to Alaska. Archeologists have found remains of 16,000 years of human habitation, revealed in tools, pots, and fishing implements. The draw for these prehistoric people? Salmon coming in from the great pasture of the Pacific.

As the ice from the last Ice Age began to melt, the water above the Columbia was held back in the mountains by a huge ice dam half a mile high, forming an inland sea called Lake Missoula in what is now western Montana. This body of water was about half the size of today's Lake Michigan. As the glaciers continued to melt, the water rose higher and higher until finally it broke through the ice dam and came crashing down into the Columbia Basin.

Within a few days, an estimated 380 cubic miles of water swept to the southwest, a wall of water 200 to 500 feet high speeding at 30 to 50 miles an hour. The deluge—called the Bretz Floods, after J. Harlen Bretz, the scientist who discovered them—carried ice, rocks, and other glacial debris as it roared into what is now Washington and Oregon with the force of a volcano. During the flood, the Columbia River held 10 times as much water as all the rivers on earth today: It was 60 times larger than the Amazon River.

"How can we conceive of the force contained in this water mass?" ask the authors of *Cataclysms on the Columbia*, a book describing the Bretz discovery.

> Imagine water blasted from a fire hose, but think of this hose as having a nozzle as wide and tall as the valleys or channels through which the flood burst. The torrent, rushing from Lake Missoula down through the Wallula Gap, ravaged and swallowed everything that lay in its path—a cornucopia gone mad, pouring forth destruction.[2]

At flood stage, the area around what is now Spokane, Washington, was buried under 500 feet of water. The glacial lake poured over the Columbia Basin, scouring and scooping out new channels along the way. As the water receded, new lakes and ponds were left behind. Finally, they too dried out, and today these channels can still be seen in eastern Washington: The once-smooth lava plains are now deeply scarred into narrow, dried-out channels called "coulees," a term adapted from the French word *couler*, meaning "to flow."

The biggest channel of them all is Grand Coulee, a 50-mile-long trench ranging from one to six miles wide and up to 900 feet deep, located south of today's Columbia River in eastern Washington. The Grand Coulee Dam turned the coulee into a reservoir, but before the dam was built, near the middle of the coulee there was a vertical escarpment 300 feet tall and extending for nearly 15 miles. During the Bretz Floods, these cliffs—for many years called "Dry Falls"—formed the largest waterfall ever to exist on the surface of the earth. The falls were five times as wide as Niagara Falls, with water 200 feet deep plunging over the precipice.

After the Bretz Floods washed over the Columbia Basin, they powered toward the Pacific in ever more narrow channels. The water rammed through the Wallula Gap at 50 miles an hour and at a depth of 1,250 feet and then descended into the Columbia River Gorge, cutting away at the channel and widening the gap in the mountains. Finally, the waters fell into the basin below the gorge, spreading out over what is now Portland and Vancouver to a depth of 400 feet. The waters backed up into the Willamette River, flooding the valley all the way south to what is now Eugene, Oregon.

The Bretz Floods occurred not just once or even twice. They came every 40 or 50 years over the course of two millennia as the glaciers melted, ice dams formed, and the dams broke, sending huge volumes of water gushing out of the mountains like giant-size buckets thrown onto the back of the Columbia Basin. By the time the floods dried up, the Columbia River had taken its current course, bending around the hard volcanic rock of the Columbia Basin, leaving innumerable coulees gouged out in its wake and then narrowing and surging through the Cascade Range to the Pacific.

No doubt the Bretz Floods wiped out whatever human habitation clung to the banks of the Columbia, as well as many of the animals that roamed the area. Then, whatever survived the floods faced the threat of a changing climate as the earth warmed and the lakes dried out. The sea also rose with the melting of the glaciers, and ocean waters flowed in to cover the coastal plains.

Native Americans drifted into the area after the great floods. They hunted the declining herds of mastodon, wooly mammoth and long-haired bison, as well as the prehistoric horses and camels. But hunting became more difficult, the Native Americans found fishing more bountiful. The new channels and rapids formed by the floods proved to be ideal fishing grounds, none more so than Celilo Falls on the east side of the Cascades, which became a prime fishing area and meeting place for many tribes in the region.

A number of old Indian tales refer to a great flood, which, according to at least one legend, grew out of family troubles among the old animal gods. People were saved from the deluge only when large birds carried them to the tops of the mountains. All the Indian legends, and the numerous variations of them, go back to the river and the seminal influence the Columbia had in their lives. According to one Indian story, the human race itself began on the Columbia River, from a large monster that once lived near the fishing grounds at Celilo Falls.

The monster was sucking in all living things with its huge hot breath. Finally, one of the prominent figures in the Indian pantheon, the god Coyote, confronted the monster and cut into its stomach. Coyote found people in the shape of animals, who had been trapped inside. These animal people were weak and emaciated, but once the monster fell, they burst out into the world and scattered themselves across the land.

Those who came from the monster's head raced to the north and became the Flathead tribe. The people from the monster's feet turned to the east and formed the Blackfoot. Then Coyote mixed the blood of the monster with water from the river and sprinkled it as rain across the valley of the Clearwater River. From these drops of blood, the Nez Percé tribe emerged.

Coyote named the people and gave them their language. He taught all the people how to fish with nets and spears along the river. He taught them that they did not have dominion over the river but rather lived as children adopted by the river. He said that the river would protect them, instruct them, and, when necessary, discipline them with fire and water. Eventually, promised the Coyote, he would return to Earth with all the spirits of the dead people and everyone would be together on the river and the world would be happy once again.

Search for a
Secret Passage

Among the Europeans, rumors flew about this river right from the beginning. People talked of a Great River, a secret passage leading from the Atlantic Ocean across the new untamed continent all the way to the Pacific. As early as 1500, only eight years after Columbus discovered America, a Portuguese sailor conceived of a Northwest Passage. In the 1500s, as Spanish and English seafarers began to explore along the west coast of the New World, they added to the myth, imagining a river leading to a splendid city along a passage to the great South Sea.

The notorious English explorer and ex-pirate Sir Francis Drake was one who sailed up the west coast of North America in the late 1500s. He got as far as what is now the Oregon coast, but he found no river, no secret passage, and he turned back, scoffing at "the most vile, thicke and stinking fogges" blanketing the area.[3] Juan de Fuca, sailing under the Spanish flag, followed on Drake's heels. He never found a river, either, but he did locate the entranceway to Puget Sound, now called the Strait of Juan de Fuca.

Meanwhile, for years, intrepid French voyageurs paddled their canoes through the watery wilderness of Canada, searching farther and farther west. Surely, they thought, even if mountains blocked the way, there would only be a short overland portage between the headwaters of the Mississippi or the farthest reaches of the Great Lakes and a river that would open the way through the hills and forests to the great expanse of the Pacific.

In 1673, two French Canadian explorers, Father Jacques Marquette and Louis Joliet, arrived at the confluence of the Mississippi and the Missouri Rivers, and they proposed that by searching out the source of these rivers, they would find another river that led to the Pacific. The French Canadians even drew a west-flowing river, called "Great River of the West" on their maps. They had never seen such a thing, but they had heard rumors from the Indians—and they knew it just *had* to exist. French officials began calling this imagined

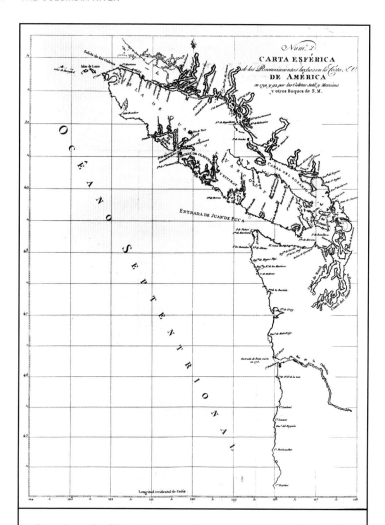

As early as the fifteenth century, Europeans, including Sir Francis Drake, Father Jacques Marquette, and Captain James Cook, navigated the Washington coast in search of a rumored Northwest Passage connecting the Atlantic Ocean and the Pacific across North America. The map shown here, from 1799, is based on the explorations of some of these European navigators. Though this mysterious passage did not actually exist, in their search for it the explorers stumbled upon other landmarks in the region as well as lucrative resources such as fish and animals for the fur trade.

territory "Ourigan," a name they adopted from the Plains Indians who spoke of such a passage.

In 1765, two years after the British won control over Canada in the French and Indian War, an expedition was proposed to travel west from Lake Superior to find the Continental Divide and the great river "Ourigan," thought to be on the other side. The expedition, led by Jonathan Carver, foundered on the Great Plains, but explorers heard yet more stories about the great river. In a 1778 book recounting his travels, Carver claimed that the Great River of the West was really the River Oregon. It rose, he said, "in about the center of this great continent" and "falls into the Pacific ocean."[4]

One fur trader sketched a map suggesting that a great river led west from northern Canada's Great Slave Lake to Cook Inlet in Alaska, which English seafarer Captain James Cook had discovered in the 1770s. Alexander MacKenzie, a Canadian explorer, later went in search of this river that does not exist. Instead, in 1789, MacKenzie found the river named after him: the MacKenzie River, which flows north through Canada and empties into the Arctic Ocean.

As overland journeys fell short of finding the Northwest Passage, explorers continued to search by sea. Captain Cook spent years roaming the Pacific Ocean. In 1778, he located the smaller Umpqua River in southern Oregon. He also touched land on what is now called Vancouver Island, British Columbia, where he purchased 1,500 beaver skins, as well as a number of sea otter pelts from the natives.

Captain Cook never found the Great River of the West, but he did discover a lucrative trade in animal furs. From the Northwest coast of America, Cook's party sailed to China, where they sold their furs for the equivalent of $100 apiece. In those days, $100 equaled two years' pay for the average seaman. Unfortunately for Cook, he never saw the profit: He was killed by natives in Hawaii. When his two ships returned to England in 1780, however, word of the valuable fur trade began to spread.

Now there was more than adventure to bring men to the Northwest coast of the New World. There was money.

Captain John Meares, a British trader eager to get in on the fur trade, used maps made by Captain Cook to sail to the Northwest, bringing along materials to build a trading post. Captain Meares stumbled on some turbulent brown waters and heavy surf and thought it might be the entrance to a big river. He could not get past the breakers because they were too rough and dangerous. He finally gave up, noting, "Disappointment continues to accompany us," and concluded that the Great River of the West was nothing but a myth: "We can now safely assert that no such River exists." [5] Although he failed to find the Northwest Passage, Meares did leave one mark on the land: The northern bank of the mouth of the Columbia River is called Cape Disappointment.

George Vancouver, who had sailed with James Cook, returned to the Northwest in the spring of 1792. He was now a captain, with three British ships under his command. His mission was to solidify British control of the area, find the Great River of the West, and map unknown parts of the coastline. Although George Vancouver did not find the Great River, he sailed around Vancouver Island, establishing that this land, which Cook had discovered a decade before, was not connected to the mainland. In the great spirit of pioneering, Vancouver named the island for himself.

At about the same time, a group of merchants in Boston sent Captain Robert Gray to the West Coast, his boat laden with trading goods. Gray had already sailed around the world once—the first American merchant to complete that journey. Now, in the spring of 1792, he possessed a letter from President George Washington addressed to all emperors and kings, requesting that they receive the captain with kindness and treat him in a becoming manner. The letter was also signed by Secretary of State Thomas Jefferson. Gray met up with George Vancouver off the Pacific shore. The two captains—one British, the other

American—exchanged information, but no one mentioned a Great River of the West.

A few weeks later, on May 11, 1792, a full 300 years after Christopher Columbus discovered the New World, Robert Gray's full-rigged, 212-ton ship, the *Columbia Rediva,* surfed over the sandbars and entered the river, located at north latitude 46 degrees and west longitude 122 degrees. It is not clear that Gray realized what he had found, because he was more interested in the local Indians than the river itself. "We found this to be a large river of fresh water, up which we steered," he recorded. "Vast numbers of natives came alongside."[6]

Gray traveled 15 miles up the river, stopping to trade with the Chinook natives who, Gray noted, perforated their noses and had oddly flat foreheads. He also declared this to be Columbia's river, naming the waterway, which was 10 miles wide at its mouth, after his ship. By this action, he established the "right" of the United States to the territory.

Gray found the Indians eager to trade. He bought salmon at the rate of two fish for one nail. He purchased 300 beaver skins, offering two metal spikes for each skin. He also gathered 3,000 sea otter pelts from the Indians, which he bartered for a few bolts of cloth and sheets of copper.

In fact, there were later reports from the Indians indicating that Gray may not have been the first white man they had ever seen. Stories from the Clatsop Indians, who lived at the mouth of the Columbia, told of men coming to shore in boats that had trees standing upright on them. These men—who the Indians called "Tlehonnipts," or "of those who drift ashore"[7]—fashioned knives and hatchets out of iron and made popping corn in iron kettles. These seafarers might have been Chinese or Japanese or even Russian but more likely they were Spaniards. Although there is no Western account of any such landing or shipwreck, one thing was for sure: When Gray met the local Indians, they were aware of white people and their metal wares and were familiar with the concept of trading.

After making his deals, Gray set out to cross the Pacific to Asia, where he would sell his sea otter skins to Chinese lords. On his way to open ocean, Gray met up with Vancouver again. The British captain had been sailing around Puget Sound. Now, as Gray continued west and Vancouver headed south for California, one of Vancouver's other ships, *The Chatham*, commanded by Lieutenant William Broughton, pushed up the newly found Columbia River.

Broughton and his men proceeded 100 miles upriver, past the point at which one of the Columbia's main tributaries, the Willamette, empties into the main river. When Vancouver later reported on his voyage, the British captain claimed that his lieutenant "formally took possession of the river and the country" in the name of King George, "having reason to believe that the subjects of no other civilized nation or state had ever entered the river before."[8]

Now there were two claims on this territory, one from the United States made in May 1792 and the other from England made in October 1792. Vancouver claimed that Gray never entered the river but only sailed around the bay. At this stage, however, no one was arguing the point. Sovereignty was not the issue at the time. People were much more interested in profits brought by trading animal skins.

There was one significant person who did, however, appreciate the foothold made by an American on the Pacific coast: Thomas Jefferson, secretary of state under George Washington and soon to be president himself. Jefferson had wanted to send an expedition to the West for a long time, proposing the idea as early as 1783. He was intrigued by reports of prehistoric creatures roaming the great empty space on the map. More important, he wanted to know if any river might provide a usable trade route to the Pacific and the Far East.

When news arrived that Gray had discovered the mouth of the Columbia, it only fueled Jefferson's ambition. The next year, 1793, Alexander MacKenzie, along with a small band of Canadian voyageurs from the Northwest Fur Company, reached the Pacific by crossing the Continental Divide in Canada. It was clear that theirs was no commercial route: The mountains were too high and the rivers too narrow.

The fur trade blossomed in the Northwest as both American and British ships plied these waters and brought their wares to the Far East. Nobody dared try to establish overland trade: It was too far, too dangerous, too foreign.

But, a few years later, after Thomas Jefferson became president, another event occurred that rekindled the idea of an overland expedition to the West. President Jefferson dispatched envoys to Paris to buy the city of New Orleans in order to secure the entrance to the Mississippi River for American traders. What the envoys got instead was an offer to sell all of the Louisiana Territory to the United States. The ambassadors made the Louisiana Purchase for $15 million, signing the deal on May 18, 1803.

With this stroke of a pen, they bought a huge tract of land running from the Gulf of Mexico to the Continental Divide of the northern Rockies (it did *not* include the Columbia River Basin of the Northwest). When Jefferson found out what had happened in Paris, he was delighted. He was getting rid of the French in North America and at the same time more than doubling the size of the United States.

Although this deal was not without its critics—one Bostonian remarked, "We are to give money of which we have too little for land of which we have too much"[9]—it was generally considered a stroke of genius, opening the rest of the continent to American expansion. Jefferson recognized the urgent need to survey this new territory. He had already signed on his secretary, Meriwether Lewis, to undertake a western expedition, and Lewis had recruited his old army captain, William Clark, as a partner.

When Lewis received the official go-ahead, he reportedly departed from Washington in such a hurry that he left his wallet behind. Jefferson supposedly forwarded the wallet to Pittsburgh, where Lewis was stopping on his way to his embarkation point in St. Louis. While in Pennsylvania, Lewis also received a letter from President Jefferson, dated June 30, 1803, with his instructions:

> The object of your mission is to explore the Missouri river, & such principal stream of it, as, by its course and communication with the waters of the Pacific ocean, whether the Columbia, Oregan, Colorado or any other river may offer the most direct & practicable water communication across the continent for the purposes of commerce.[10]

Lewis and Clark and their Corps of Discovery left St. Louis on May 14, 1804. They struggled up the Missouri River and wintered in the Dakotas, where they joined up with Toussaint Charbonneau, a French guide, and his Indian wife, Sacagawea, who was pregnant.

The next spring, the expedition proceeded by dugout canoe and then on foot up into the Rocky Mountains until, exhausted and almost starving, they found the Continental Divide. As Lewis, leader of the advance party, recorded on August 12, 1805,

> They arrived at the top of a ridge from which they saw high mountains, partially covered with snow, still to the west of them. The ridge on which they stood formed the dividing line between the waters of the Atlantic and the Pacific Oceans. They found the descent much steeper than on the eastern side, and at the distance of three-quarters of a mile, reached a handsome, bold creek of cold, clear water running to the westward. They stopped to taste for the first time the waters of the Columbia.[11]

The moment must have meant both good news and bad news for Meriwether Lewis. He had finally found the headwaters of the Missouri River and climbed the Continental Divide. The bad news: Instead of looking out at some great river extending to the South Seas, he saw, as Lewis himself described, "immence ranges of high mountains still to the West of us with their tops partially covered with snow."[12]

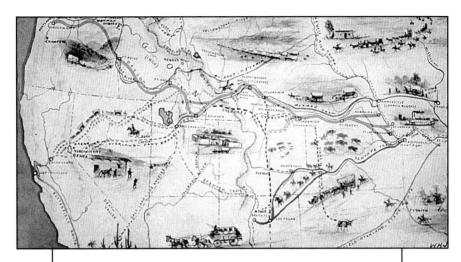

In 1804, after purchasing the Louisiana Territory from France, President Thomas Jefferson sent Meriwether Lewis and William Clark to explore the unfamiliar area. They traveled from St. Louis, Missouri, across the Continental Divide and down the Columbia River to the Pacific Ocean. Lewis and Clark's Corps of Discovery not only charted the new territory for President Jefferson, but it also paved the way for the pioneers who would soon begin traveling to the frontier via the Westward Trail, depicted here as it appeared in 1840.

Good news soon followed. Lewis met up with a band of Blackfoot Indians. He explained his predicament and said that there was an Indian woman in their party. By coincidence, it turned out that the Blackfoot chief was Sacagawea's brother, who she had not seen since being captured in a raid as a young girl.

The Blackfoot supplied the explorers with horses. Lewis went back over the mountains, retrieved the rest of the Corps of Discovery, and continued west over a snowy Continental Divide. The Lewis and Clark party stumbled through the Bitterroot Range of the Rocky Mountains and found the Clearwater River. Leaving their horses with a band of Nez Percé Indians, who would take care of them until the expedition returned the next year, Lewis and Clark paused to carve five canoes from the trees

A WET WINTER AT FORT CLATSOP

When the Corps of Discovery reached the mouth of the Columbia, Lewis and Clark made camp on the north shore of the river, where they traded with the Clatsop Indians and tried in vain to keep dry in the constant rain. Clark noted that the men were "as wet as water could make them," and a few days later complained, "O! how horrible is the day, waves brakeing with great violence against the Shore throwing the Water into our Camp &c. all wet and confined to our shelters."*

To decide where to make a more permanent winter camp, the two expedition leaders put it to a vote. The explorers had heard that hunting was better on the south side of the river—and they thought the weather might be a little drier—so the vote was decisive. They would move.

They crossed the Columbia in their dugout canoes and found a site seven miles inland from the ocean on the bank of a small stream that empties into the Columbia. The men built an encampment of log cabins and soon were huddled inside their huts trying to stay dry and warm.

Their accommodations were hardly luxurious. Christmas dinner consisted of spoiled elk meat, some pounded fish, and a few roots. The men were able to repair their weapons; they mended their clothes, hunted for deer and elk, and traded with the Indians. They made several trips to the coast to distill salt from seawater—they would use the salt to cure meat for the return journey.

Unknown to Lewis and Clark, an American ship was in the vicinity that winter of 1805–6, trading along the Northwest coast. Lewis and Clark were aware that American ships plied these waters, but they never got wind of this ship or made contact with any other Americans. On March 23, it was time to leave, to reach the Rockies by June when the mountain passes would be open.

Today, a few miles southwest of Astoria, Oregon, on the site of the original Fort Clatsop, you can visit a reproduction of Lewis and Clark's winter camp, their home for three months. The reproduction was built in 1955 for the sesquicentennial (150-year) celebration of that original winter experience. The 125-acre site, now administered as part of the National Park Service, is open every day of the year except Christmas. It features a 50-by-50-foot replica of Fort Clatsop, along with a canoe landing on the nearby Lewis and Clark River. In Seaside, Oregon, a few miles away on the coast, you can see an exhibit of the camp where members of the expedition boiled seawater to make salt to cure their fish and meat.

* Quoted in Snyder, *In the Footsteps of Lewis & Clark*, 164–65.

growing by the river. They then descended the Clearwater, which on October 10 brought them to the Snake River. They floated down the Snake for 120 miles to the junction of the Snake and the Columbia Rivers, where they were met by 200 Indians. William Clark was astonished at the bounty brought in by the river, noting that "the number of dead Salmon on the Shores & floating in the river is incredible to see—and at this season they [the Indians] have only to collect them."[13]

Lewis and Clark paddled down the Columbia, where as many as 100 rapids then existed. They portaged their canoes around the worst of the rapids, but ran The Dalles, or "the chute," where the Columbia narrowed to only 150 feet wide and the water ran fast and furious. On November 7, 1805, William Clark, paddling through the mist on the ever-widening river, finally spied the Pacific Ocean. "Ocean in view," he cried out. "O! the joy!"[14]

The expedition wintered at the mouth of the Columbia with the Clatsop Indians—four months of nonstop rain, it was noted. The Indians were accustomed to trading with Europeans and had even picked up some English words such as "musket," "powder" and "damned rascal."

On March 23, 1806, Lewis and Clark started back up the Columbia for their return trip. The adventurers picked up their horses from the Nez Percé, rode back over the Continental Divide, and then floated down the Missouri River, arriving in St. Louis on September 26, 1806. Lewis and Clark's mission was a success: They mapped the Louisiana Territory, brought home information about myriad new plants and animals, and finally discovered the Great River of the West.

The Great River proved to be no secret passage to the Pacific. In fact, with Lewis and Clark, the 300-year-old myth of a water route across North America was shattered once and for all. However, the river that Captain Robert Gray entered by mouth and Lewis and Clark by mountain, would fulfill another promise for the fledging country.

3

Early Settlement

By the time the Europeans arrived, the Columbia River had already been settled for hundreds, perhaps thousands, of years. Native Americans fished the river and its tributaries, hunted deer and elk, and foraged for berries and other wild foods.

These original settlers of the Columbia River fell into two broad groups. West of the Cascades were the Chinook, Clatsop, Multnomah, and Willamette tribes, totaling perhaps 15,000 people. Hemmed in by the dense fir forests, they settled in villages and provided for themselves by fishing for salmon in the river. They lived in wooden houses, with several families to a house. A fire in the center of the house helped keep them warm. A hole in the roof let out some of the smoke; what remained hovered underneath the eaves and cured the fish hanging from the ceiling.

East of the Cascades lived 30,000 plateau Indians, who rode horses, as did the tribes of the Great Plains. These were the Cayuse, Walla Walla, Yakima, Umatilla, Spokane, Shoshone, Flathead, and Nez Percé. They moved with the seasons, fishing on the river during salmon runs, gathering berries and hunting game on the plateau at other times. Some were fur trappers; others were savvy traders. Some of these Indians made excursions over the Continental Divide to hunt and trade on the Great Plains.

These tribes traditionally came together in the Columbia River Gorge to trade and feast and exchange news. In all, there were perhaps 50,000 to 70,000 Indians living in the Columbia River watershed, as the nineteenth century began, a level not reached by whites until after the Civil War.

Farther north, in what is now Canada, the Kootenay Indians hunted and fished in the Columbia valley, which was protected by the surrounding mountains and enjoyed relatively moderate weather and rainfall. Salmon migrated from the Pacific all the way to Columbia Lake at the source of the river. The marshy valley was also home to a bounty of birds and wildlife, including ducks and geese, as well as beaver, mountain goats, deer, sheep, and bears.

The first white people to arrive were the explorers led by English, Spanish, and American seafarers. Soon, commerce took over as the allure of the beaver and sea otter turned explorers into

Native Americans, seen here fishing for salmon at Kettle Falls in Washington, in an 1846 painting, had inhabited the land surrounding the Columbia River for hundreds of years before American, Canadian, and European settlers arrived in the early nineteenth century. Despite some strained relations with the Native American tribes and harsh environmental conditions, settlers soon established successful villages and trading posts.

traders and brought in trappers in search of what they called "hairy money." Reports filtered back to the East Coast about the profits made by John Gray and other traders, and ambitious Americans wanted to get in on the bonanza. John Jacob Astor was among the first.

Astor had emigrated from Germany at the end of the American Revolution and made his fortune shipping goods, including furs, from the New World to England. When he heard about the opportunities around the Columbia River, he approached the Northwest Fur Company in Montreal to form a partnership. The Northwest Company was a young upstart of a trading company set up by Canadians of French and Scottish heritage to compete with the more established Hudson's Bay Company of England, which enjoyed exclusive trading rights over the watershed of Hudson Bay. The Northwest Company, which had its own emissaries exploring the Columbia, turned down Astor's proposal. Astor organized his own partnership, hired several traders from Canada, and began preparations to send an expedition to the Pacific.

A group of 50 Astorians, under the command of Astor partner Wilson Price Hunt, set out for Oregon by land in 1810. Others went by sea in two ships, the *Tonquin* and the *Beaver,* to carry the supplies for a permanent fur-trading post on the Columbia River. The *Tonquin* was first to arrive, in March 1811. The ship encountered trouble immediately.

The weather was stormy as the *Tonquin* approached the mouth of the river. The captain nevertheless ordered a boat to be put into the water to sound out the channel. The boat, with five men aboard, disappeared into the waves and was never seen again. The next day, another craft was launched, again to be tossed by the waves until it disappeared.

That evening, the *Tonquin* itself ran aground on a sandbar. The ship was saved only when the tide flooded in and tossed the vessel over the bar and into safe harbor. The next day, the captain went in search of his lost men and found one sailor who was wet and naked and suffering intensely from the cold. A second man also survived. Eight people lost their lives trying to cross the Columbia Bar.

The survivors landed on the south shore of the river and began to cut down trees to build their Astoria post. Soon they decided to send an expedition upriver to explore the territory and look for representatives of the Northwest Fur Company, called Nor'westers. According to the Indians, Nor'westers were already trading along the river, and just as the Americans were ready to leave, a canoe flying the British flag came into view. A man named David Thompson leaped ashore.

Thompson, a Nor'wester himself, reported that he had crossed the Canadian Rockies the year before and wintered near the headwaters of the Columbia. Now he was making the journey to the Pacific. David Thompson was in fact the first person in recorded history to make the 1,200-mile voyage from the headwaters of the Columbia to the Pacific.

Thompson had opened a number of small trading posts along the Upper Columbia and its tributaries, including the first trading post west of the Rocky Mountains, called Kootenai House, and another on the Spokane River, which would later become the most influential post in the Columbia Basin. He had come to set up a trading fort at the mouth of the river. Because the Americans were already there, Thompson went back up the river and continued to expand his trade in the interior, securing the allegiance of the Indians and extending the reach of the Northwest Company.

The Astor party went ahead with a journey into the interior that summer, erecting an American trading post where the Okanogan River empties into the Columbia, 540 miles above Astoria. Just as the Americans and the British had competed over the discovery of the Columbia back in 1792, they were now beginning to compete with each other for the fur trade.

In the fall of 1811, the local Indians, the Chinook, grew increasingly distrustful of the Americans, perhaps because they were beginning to realize the white people were there to stay. Duncan McDougall, the Astoria partner acting as head of the post, heard of disquiet among the Indians and came up with a brilliant if devious response. He learned that a few years before, the Indians had suffered from an outbreak of smallpox. They were terrified of the disease.

McDougall called together several of the chiefs and showed them a small vial. "I am the great smallpox chief," he told them. "In this little bottle I keep the smallpox. If I uncork the bottle and let it out I will kill every man, woman and child of the Indians. Now go in peace, but if you make war upon us I will open the bottle and you will die."[15]

The Chinooks believed his ruse and left the Astorians alone.

Unfortunately, as often happens, the deception came back to haunt them. A few years later, an outbreak of smallpox ravaged Indians farther upriver, and they believed that the Americans had released the disease on purpose, causing further friction between the Indians and these aggressive new immigrants.

Meanwhile, at Astoria, to cement peaceful acceptance by the Indians, McDougall took one more step: He married the daughter of Comcomly, chief of the Chinooks. The Indians and the whites joined in the wedding celebration, and Comcomly's daughter became first lady of the Columbia.

In the winter of 1811–12, the party led by Wilson Price Hunt struggled into Astoria. They had trekked over the Rocky Mountains, braving the cold, the snow, the wind, and the dangerous waters. Several lives were lost to starvation and drowning, but now the new settlement on the Columbia, called Fort Astoria, was taking root.

In May 1812, the second Astoria ship arrived, bringing additional equipment and supplies. More men were sent upriver to establish an American trading post where the Spokane River meets the Columbia, and another trading party explored up the Snake River. Despite difficulties, the Astoria venture seemed to be on the verge of success.

It was not to be. First, the *Tonquin*, which had been sent to trade up along the Pacific coast toward Vancouver Island, was destroyed by hostile tribes. Word came that a third Astoria ship, sailing from New York, was lost at sea. Then news arrived that the United States and England had gone to war—the War of 1812. The Astoria partners, several of whom were Canadian, voted to sell out to the Northwest Company. McDougall became head of the fort under the Canadians. Soon after the transfer occurred, a British man-of-war sailed into the Columbia River to take the fort, only to find that it had already been given up. The British renamed the outpost Fort George.

When the War of 1812 ended, the Treaty of Ghent provided for territory taken by either side to be restored to its original owner. The fur-trading outpost on the Columbia therefore was returned

John Jacob Astor was one of the first Americans to send a venture to the Columbia River region, with hopes of increasing his fortune through the lucrative fur trade. His expedition was ill-fated, however, and his fur trading post of Astoria, seen here in 1813, was taken over by the Northwest Fur Company after the start of the War of 1812.

to the United States, but the partnership of John Jacob Astor had ceased operations, so the Northwest Company was allowed to remain at Fort George.

The Nor'westers opened more posts along the Columbia and its tributaries. Despite occasional strained relations with the Americans and a few flare-ups with Indians throughout the region, Canadians controlled the Columbia for the next three decades, until the mid-1840s, supplying trading posts from Astoria up north to Canada and reaping handsome profits from the furs they sent back to the East Coast as well as to China and Europe.

In 1821, the Northwest Fur Company merged with the bigger, stronger Hudson's Bay Company, further cementing the Canadian grip on the Northwest. Three years later, George Simpson, governor of northern operations for Hudson's Bay Company, arrived at Fort George with some new plans. He appointed Dr. John

McLoughlin chief factor of the post (a Hudson's Bay trading post was called a "factory" and the head of it the "chief factor"). He also directed McLoughlin to move headquarters of the trading post to Fort Vancouver, across the river from where the Willamette enters the Columbia, about 100 miles upstream. Today, this is Vancouver, Washington, located across the river from Portland, Oregon.

McLoughlin took this opportunity to expand the trading post. He built a stockade fort about as big as a football field, with a store, several warehouses, a number of homes, and a school for the children of Hudson's Bay employees. He also encouraged people to clear fields around the fort and plant gardens to supplement provisions brought in by ship. Within a few years, the Hudson's Bay Company had also brought in cattle, sheep, and horses. Once a year, a ship would arrive from England, circling around Cape Horn and crossing the dangerous Columbia Bar, to bring supplies to Hudson's Bay employees. Also every year, a group of traders would paddle up the Columbia to Boat Encampment, a settlement at the northernmost tip of the river in what is now British Columbia. The men would store their boats, transfer to horses, and cross the Canadian Rockies to Winnipeg. They would then return with supplies and mail and word from home for the Canadians.

The Hudson's Bay Company promoted agriculture to lessen reliance on imports, and farming thrived on the prairie surrounding Fort Vancouver. In 1826 Lieutenant Emilius Simpson came to Fort Vancouver from London and brought with him a packet of apple seeds. The results were an immediate success: One visitor was impressed by

> the apples, which grow on small trees, the branches of which would be broken without the support of props. So profuse is the quantity of fruit that the limbs are covered with it, and it is actually packed together precisely in the same manner that onions are attached to ropes when they are exposed for sale in our markets.[16]

John McLoughlin presented an imposing figure at six feet four inches tall and with a mane of long white hair. Traders and

Even though its waters were treacherous, the Columbia River was an important factor in the settlement of the Northwest. The area around the river provided transportation, and many natural resources and opportunities to make money harvesting fish, trapping beaver and sea otter, and trading furs. The river is still significant today as a commercial waterway for cargo ships, like the one shown here, and as a provider of irrigation and electricity through its dams.

Indians alike called him "Old Whitehead" or "White Eagle." The son of an Irish farmer who had emigrated to Canada, McLoughlin pursued medical studies in Quebec before casting his lot with the fur traders. He was now in a position of great power, because the profits from the fur trade were immense. One trader, for example, reported that he collected 1,550 beaver skins, plus various other pelts, and paid in goods and cash the equivalent of approximately $56. When they were sold in China these furs brought in $3,600—a profit of more than 6,000 percent!

McLoughlin himself lived in a two-story home behind the 20-foot-high stockade. He ran the fort with a stern hand, ringing bells at shift changes. Workmen were given strict rations. Anyone—Indian or white man—caught breaking the rules would likely receive a whipping while lashed to the fort's cannon. Officers lived a more civilized existence, with elaborate dinners served in a candlelit officer's mess hall. Entertainment included singing and dancing and bagpipes.

In order to keep the fur trade under control of the Hudson's Bay Company, McLoughlin discouraged Americans from migrating to the Columbia. At that time, the United States extended only to the Rocky Mountains—the limit of the Louisiana Purchase—and all the territory west of the mountains was divided into two parts: California, which was claimed by Mexico, and to the north, Oregon, which was disputed by England and the United States. The understanding was that Oregon would ultimately belong to the country that settled it first.

When American immigrants began to arrive, McLoughlin and his Hudson's Bay colleagues were polite, sometimes even helping them by providing food and other supplies. They discouraged Americans from settling around Fort Vancouver, however. McLoughlin befriended American mountain man Jedediah Smith, one of those who discovered the South Pass that later proved to be the key to the Oregon Trail. When Smith was attacked by the Umpqua Indians and all but two of his party were killed, McLoughlin gave Smith help and sent out a party to get back the furs. Yet when Nathaniel Wyeth, a Boston merchant, arrived to build an American trading post on the Columbia, McLoughlin reacted quickly, paying the Indians a higher price for their furs to drive Wyeth out of business.

The Canadians, already worried about the influx of Americans, thought that if they steered the newcomers south of the river, then when it came time to settle the international boundary, the Americans might be content to draw the line at the Columbia. Many of the first Americans followed McLoughlin's advice and headed south into the Willamette Valley, where the weather was milder and the fields more fertile. Some of the missionaries followed suit. When one settler journeyed south to California and led a cattle drive back into the Willamette Valley, the Americans began to develop pasturelands along the Willamette and its tributaries. By 1840, an informal census had counted 200 people living in the Willamette Valley, 137 Americans and 63 Canadians.

In 1844, when McLoughlin finally resigned from the Hudson's Bay Company, the factor himself moved to the Willamette Valley, building a house in newly formed Oregon City. Today, the main reason that Oregon has English names like Portland and Salem and Washington has Indian names like Seattle, Walla Walla, and Yakima, is that many more whites settled into the Willamette Valley at an earlier stage. The Americans also brought their diseases—such as smallpox and measles—with them, which killed off the Indians in Oregon sooner and more completely than those farther north.

Before McLoughlin left the Hudson's Bay Company, he expanded and improved its network of trading posts east of the Cascades, along the Columbia and its tributaries. In 1821, David Thompson's Spokane outpost was moved to nearby Fort Spokane and then a few years later regional headquarters was again moved, this time to Fort Colville, above Kettle Falls, in a valley protected from the worst of winter winds. The new trading post, perhaps the most important Hudson's Bay post on the Columbia outside of Fort Vancouver, was protected by a block-house and a high picket fence and sported a blacksmith shop and a carpenter's shop, as well as storage areas and rooms for visitors.

Kettle Falls was already a favorite fishing spot where Indians congregated to catch salmon, using baskets to collect the fish that fell back from the falls. Fort Colville attracted Indian visitors, as well as hunters, trappers, and traders who might need provisions or who just wanted to see a friendly face.

There were two kinds of trappers. The voyageurs from Canada were sociable people who lived on or near the river, knew every rapid and whirlpool, and navigated even the most dangerous sections of the Columbia with skill and intensity. Voyageurs routinely ran the rapids of the Columbia, portaging only around Kettle Falls and Celilo Falls. They paddled log canoes, hollowed out from fir trees that grew along the banks of the river. The boats, about 50 feet long, could hold up to 20 people and three tons of cargo. Others used craft called bateaux, which were typically

5 feet wide and 30 feet long, propelled with oars and steered with paddles. They were roomier than the canoes but had shallow drafts so they could be maneuvered on the river even when fully loaded—and they were light enough to be portaged around the waterfalls.

The other trappers were the famous mountain men. They were British or American rather than French and spent less time on the river and more time wandering alone into forests to find their furs. These trappers were more independent than the voyageurs and relied on guns rather than their charm and wits for survival.

All the trappers and traders were tough, taking the inevitable hardships in stride. One trapper was famous for joking about playing cards in the wintry mountains with three other men—using a frozen corpse as their card table. Another famous mountain man, Jim Bridger, lived for many months with a three-inch metal arrowhead stuck in his back. It was finally removed by the missionary Dr. Marcus Whitman. When the doctor wondered why the wound hadn't become infected, Bridger replied gruffly, "Meat jes don't spoil in the mountains." [17]

Yet, it was there American fur trappers like Jim Bridger, who roamed far and wide on both sides of the Rocky Mountains and finally found the key to the West. With help from their Indian friends, they discovered a broad and relatively gentle route through the mountains far to the south of where Lewis and Clark had made their crossing. It rose gently through the Continental Divide at only 7,500 feet and was used by American trappers who competed with the Hudson's Bay Company. South Pass would soon provide the route for thousands of settlers who now had a way to bring their wagons and supplies over the high Rocky Mountains. These were the pioneers who walked off in search of America along the famous Oregon Trail.

4

The Americans
Are Coming

The monopoly of the Hudson's Bay Company was never threatened by any competitor or military force. Instead, it was the constant and growing influx of American settlers and missionaries who literally overran the territory and then cried out for recognition, political stability, and, eventually, government services.

Interest in "the Ory-gon" was stoked first by explorers and mountain men who went back east with accounts of the mild climate and fertile farmland in the Northwest and then by the missionaries, who set out to convert the Indians and came back to recruit American immigrants to expand their efforts. Mountain man Jedediah Smith reported to the secretary of war as early as 1830 that it was possible to take wagons and herds of cattle across the mountains by way of South Pass, along what was to become the Oregon Trail.

One early explorer was Captain Benjamin L.E. Bonneville, a French American graduate of West Point who in 1832 organized a fur trading company. He traveled to Oregon through the South Pass and across Idaho. Though Bonneville's fur business never got anywhere, he returned to New York and met writer Washington Irving at the home of John Jacob Astor. As a result of this meeting, Irving wrote a tale, *The Adventures of Captain Bonneville*, which together with another Irving book, *Astoria: Adventure in the Pacific Northwest*, recounting the multimillionaire's ambitious attempt in the fur trade, stoked interest in the future of Columbia country.

In 1831, a group of Nez Percé and Flathead Indians who had been impressed by the white man's technology made their way to St. Louis and asked to see the "white-man's book" that could tell them how to worship the Great Spirit. When this request was made public, a number of religious groups quickly became interested in sending missionaries to convert the Indians. A Methodist minister, Jason Lee, along with his nephew, Daniel Lee, set out to bring Christianity to the Flathead tribe, joining a westward voyage led by Nathaniel Wyeth in 1834. Lee ended up continuing on to the Willamette Valley, where he set up a mission at Oregon City.

The most famous and influential missionary of the time,

however, was Marcus Whitman, the doctor who patched up the wounded Jim Bridger. In 1836, with his new wife, Narcissa, and several compatriots, Dr. Whitman journeyed from upstate New York first to St. Louis and then across the Great Plains and Rocky Mountains to the Columbia. Included in the party was fellow Presbyterian missionary Henry Spalding, who had previously asked Narcissa to marry him. Narcissa had refused Spalding, and he had married another woman. The two couples were committed to converting the Indians, and so they traveled together. Narcissa Whitman and Eliza Spalding were the first white women to make the overland trek to Oregon.

The Whitman group traversed South Pass, arriving at the Hudson's Bay Company fort at the mouth of the Walla Walla River, which joins the Columbia just below the Snake, on September 2, 1836. Dr. Whitman then proceeded down to Fort Vancouver, where he met Dr. McLoughlin, his fellow doctor and adventurer. Because Jason Lee had already set up a Methodist mission in the Willamette Valley, Whitman and Spalding both went back upriver.

The Spaldings decided to preach to the Nez Percé and started a mission at Lapwai, on the Clearwater River, a tributary of the Snake in what is now western Idaho. The Whitmans settled among the Cayuse, about 100 miles from Lapwai, at a place called *Waiilatpu,* which means "the place of rye grass which grows on the hills."[18] In the distance, to the southeast, were the Blue Mountains, where settlers came en route from the East. For a while, the Whitman mission was the gateway to Oregon.

The Whitmans built a crude house for themselves on the Walla Walla, about 25 miles upriver from the Hudson's Bay fort. Dr. Whitman began to preach to the Cayuse. Narcissa became pregnant, had a daughter, and was soon running a nursery school for Cayuse children. When the Whitmans' daughter was just two years old, however, she fell into the river and drowned. Then two Cayuse brothers in Narcissa's school got sick and died. Then, Narcissa herself came down with an illness.

The Cayuse were not particularly responsive to Dr. Whitman's Presbyterian teachings. When Whitman preached that because they were not Christians the Cayuse would not be saved, the Indians were offended. They told Whitman he should not use "bad talk" to threaten them.

As more whites filtered into the area, the Cayuse became increasingly wary of Whitman's intentions. On several occasions, the Cayuse suggested that Whitman should pay them for the land where he had built his house. Meanwhile, Dr. Whitman became increasingly frustrated with his lack of success in converting the Indians. As time went on, he focused his attentions more on the new settlers arriving from the East.

In 1841, as the Cayuse pressed the question of land ownership, the missionary board back east considered closing the Whitman outpost. Dr. Whitman decided to return home to save his job, leaving Narcissa to tend their new home. During the trip, Whitman stopped in Washington, D.C., to lobby for federal support. Whitman knew he needed help to fend off the Hudson's Bay Company, which was trying to discourage immigration into the Northwest, and to overcome resistance from Indians who did not welcome his missionary message.

Whitman told President Tyler and others that wagons could be taken to Oregon, and he argued in favor of establishing forts along the trail out west. Also, during his trip, Dr. Whitman recruited 900 settlers to return with him to Oregon. This journey in the summer of 1843 became known as the Great Migration, because it was the first mass movement of settlers to the Columbia. These people would help Whitman establish a stronger American presence in Oregon and give him more souls to save at his mission.

Meanwhile, Oregon stayed on the political agenda in Washington, D.C. Conservatives from New England cast a dim view on westward expansion, realizing that this vast area threatened to eclipse the power of the eastern establishment. Democrats, with heavier representation in the western states of Illinois, Ohio, and Missouri, were more eager to extend American influence to the Northwest. The Democratic platform in 1844 called for "54 degrees, 40 minutes," representing the latitude they wanted to proclaim for the northern boundary of the United States—which

By the mid-nineteenth century, American interest in westward expansion and the territory in the Northwest was intense. After being elected president in 1844, James Polk declared the United States' rights to Oregon to be "clear and unquestionable." He soon signed a treaty with England, setting the U.S. northern border at the 49th parallel and establishing American dominance in the West.

would have included all the western lands north to Alaska. Senator William Allen of Ohio is credited with coming up with the slogan "Fifty-four, forty, or fight!"

Democrat James Polk was elected president that year, and he declared that the U.S. title to Oregon was "clear and unquestionable."

When England dug in its heels, moderates came to the forefront and Americans let it be known that they would compromise at the 49th parallel. A deal was made, and President Polk signed the treaty in June 1846, establishing the international boundary with Canada at the 49th parallel, where it remains today.

That same year, George Simpson of the Hudson's Bay Company bowed to the inevitable and moved his Canadian fur-trading headquarters to Victoria, British Columbia. Dr. McLoughlin took another course and retired from the Hudson's Bay Company to the shores of the Willamette.

As early as 1842, a group of men in the Willamette Valley met to form a provisional government. A committee was appointed and voted to formulate a constitution guaranteeing freedom of worship, trial by jury, and other basic civil rights. The committee also voted to encourage education and prohibit taking land from the Indians without their consent, and it stipulated that any sort of slavery should not exist. In 1843, at a meeting on the banks of the Willamette, settlers voted to form a government.

The legislative body consisted of nine people; in addition, there were several judges. Every white man over the age of 21 could vote. Marriage was allowed to males at age 16 and to females at age 14. Any individual could claim land, up to a square mile, provided it had no other claims on it. Because there were no official surveys, each land claimer marked his own territory. Soon after, an amendment to the constitution to provide for a governor was adopted, and a member of the Methodist mission, George Abernethy, was first to be chosen to occupy the position.

Meanwhile, after Whitman arrived back in Oregon in 1843, he wrote to his wife's parents:

> As I hold the settlement of this country by Americans rather than by an English colony most important, I am happy to have been the means of landing so large an emigration on to the shore of the Columbia. . . . I have no doubt our greatest work is to be to aid the white settlement of this country and help found its religious institutions.[19]

The Cayuse, however, were alarmed when they saw 900 settlers rolling down from the Blue Mountains into Oregon. They expressed relief only when they realized that most of the settlers were moving on to the Willamette. The immigrants paused at *Waiilatpu* and then stopped at Fort Walla Walla, where the Americans built flatboats to take them down the Columbia.

The settlers loaded their equipment onto the boats and floated downriver for a hundred miles without incident. When they reached The Dalles, trouble began. The risk-takers chose to run the rapids by boat; some made it, some didn't. Others elected to portage around the wildest section of the river. These people became mired in the mud and steep terrain. Fortunately, Dr. McLoughlin, at Fort Vancouver, heard of their peril. He sent help upriver, carrying food and blankets to the weary and wet travelers.

The settlers of the Great Migration finally arrived in Fort Vancouver and then headed south into the Willamette Valley, where they joined the missionaries and the motley crew of trappers and traders who lived along the river. The next spring, the settlers spread out over the valley, claiming their square mile of the American dream.

In 1840, before the Great Migration, there were only about 100 Americans living in Columbia country. Now the great waves of immigrants had begun, one wagon train after another trundling along the Oregon Trail, over the South Pass, and down the perilous Columbia through the Cascade Mountains. In 1844, three parties with a total of 1,500 people arrived in Oregon country. In 1845, 3,000 settlers made the journey.

The Oregon Trail was known by numerous landmarks, such as Chimney Rock, Laramie Peak, Independence Rock, Twin Buttes near the South Pass, Three Buttes in Idaho, and, later, Mount Hood. The trail was also marked by goods discarded by settlers who had loaded their wagons too heavily, by the carcasses of dead animals, and occasionally by a gravestone of someone who had died—usually in a gun or horse accident, occasionally by disease, and rarely by Indian attack. In 1852, the busiest year on the trail, a reported 45 people lost their lives to Indians. A few of these

ALL YOU NEED IS LOVE

Although the history of the Columbia River is dominated by the western expansion of the United States and the inevitable tide of white development, the area has also provided home to more unusual groups, perhaps because it was one of the last regions in North America to be settled. Shortly after 1900, several thousand religious dissenters from Russia settled in and around the town of Castlegar, British Columbia, near the spot where the Kootenay River meets the Columbia, just north of the Canadian border.

These people, called Doukhobors (Russian for "spirit wrestlers"), abstained from alcohol and tobacco and built no churches. They were pacifists who did not kill animals or eat meat. They believed that all men are equal, that all are brothers, and that only love is of paramount importance. Their beliefs got them into trouble first with the Russian government and later with the Canadian government, because they refused to be conscripted into an army and would not pledge allegiance to any government.

The Doukhobors, led by Peter Verigin, acquired several thousand acres along the Columbia River and set up villages with communal homes. They started their own farms and orchards and mills. Some traditional Doukhobors, however, began to worry that Verigin was too progressive, and one day in 1924, after he boarded a Canadian Pacific Railway train, a massive explosion rocked the train, killing Verigin, a female friend, and several other passengers. Was he assassinated? Some people point the finger at a man who helped Verigin onto the train with his bags, suggesting that the stranger slipped an explosive into Verigin's suitcase. Others insist that the explosion was merely an accident, pointing out that miners often carried illegal explosives onto trains, and sometimes the gaslights malfunctioned and caught on fire.

Today, many people of Russian ancestry live around Castlegar, and Doukhobor still exists as a religion. You can visit the Doukhobor Historical Village in southern British Columbia, where more than a thousand items—from clothing and arts and crafts to a wood-fired sauna—reflect the life and times of the Doukhobor culture in the early 1900s.

settlers stopped around Walla Walla or at various spots along the Columbia, but for most, the ultimate destination was the Willamette Valley, with its lush farmland and mild winters.

In 1845, to help ease the last part of the trip, a man named

S.K. Barlow laid out an alternate route to the Willamette Valley, one that took people away from the Columbia above the Cascades and circled around to the south of Mount Hood. For the first year or two the going was no better: The road was so steep that in some spots, wagons had to be guided downhill with ropes. As the road was improved, however, it became the easier route for people headed to the Willamette. Other entrepreneurs went to work on improving the portage around the Columbia rapids. Francis Chenoweth built a crude two-mile tram bypassing the rapids by 1851. The tram was later extended, easing the way for the settlers now arriving en masse.

Meanwhile, back upriver, the Whitman mission had expanded to encompass 40 acres, with herds of cattle grazing the fields. The house was much improved from its original makeshift condition: It was now two stories constructed out of whitewashed adobe. Narcissa still taught the Cayuse children, but there was no love lost between the Indians and the Whitmans. The Cayuse became more anxious as the whites streamed in, built houses, plowed farms, and brought diseases that the Indians had never seen before.

In 1847, a measles epidemic broke out along the Walla Walla River. The Indians were helpless, and when they turned to Dr. Whitman for medical help, his remedies failed. Even though several whites got sick as well, rumors began to circulate among the Indians that Dr. Whitman was poisoning them, plotting to wipe them out.

On November 29, 1847, the Whitmans were at home when a number of Indians came in asking for medicine. One Cayuse brave pulled out his hatchet and struck Whitman in the head, splitting his skull. The Indians then attacked other men in the mission, and when Narcissa came to the aid of her husband, she was shot in the chest. The Indians dragged her outside, beat her, and cut her with knives and hatchets. When the massacre was over, more than a dozen people at the mission had been killed. The Cayuse held captive a number of women and children for several days until a Hudson's Bay representative arrived and paid a ransom to free them.

As settlers flooded into the West, some Native American tribes grew increasingly hostile, concerned about the loss of their land and threats to their way of life. In 1847, one group of Cayuse Indians took action, attacking American missionary Marcus Whitman, whom they believed cheated and betrayed them. Whitman, his wife, and twelve others at the mission were murdered in what is now known as the Whitman Massacre.

This attack marked the beginning of the Cayuse War, which flared up periodically for three years. Yet the Nez Percé, the Spokane, and the Umatilla refused to join the Cayuse, and their cause eventually proved hopeless. Indeed, it was a band of friendly Umatilla who finally captured the leaders of the Cayuse. On June 3, 1850, five Cayuse warriors were hanged in Oregon City, on the Willamette River, for the murder of the Whitman party, even though there was some question whether these five men had had anything to do with that uprising.

The Indian wars, however, did not discourage people from coming to Oregon. Indeed, when Washington, D.C., heard of the Whitman massacre, six months after it occurred, the president and Congress were moved to action, officially creating Oregon Territory, which included all of what is now Washington and Idaho. More and more Americans continued to arrive from the Midwest. The peak year was 1852, when 10,000 people trekked over the Oregon Trail. In all, from 1840 to the completion of the transcontinental railroad in 1869, some 50,000 people made the journey, increasing the white population in the Northwest from a few hundred to more than 100,000.

In 1853, Congress created Washington Territory, separating it from Oregon, encompassing the present states of Washington and Idaho, as well as parts of Wyoming and Montana. A man named Isaac Stevens was appointed governor, and he decided he needed to solve the "Indian issue." His motives were not exactly pure: Stevens was also in charge of a survey team scouting a path for a railway to connect the Midwest with the Northwest. He knew that before anyone could start building a railroad, they needed land.

In 1855, Stevens convened a council at Walla Walla to negotiate with the Indian tribes living east of the Cascades. Stevens showed up with 50 men, and there were 2,500 Nez Percé, 300 Cayuse, and 2,000 Yakima, Umatilla, and Walla Walla. The American governor wanted the Indians to move to reservations designated for the various tribes. The Indians were divided over the idea. The Yakima chief called Kamiakin led the faction that was unwilling to give up Indian land to the newcomers. "Where can we go?" said Kamiakin. "Only a single mountain now separates us from the big salt water of the setting sun . . . better to die like brave warriors on the battle-field than live among our vanquishers, despised."[20] Others were prepared to bow to the inevitable and agree to the reservations.

The council went on for over a week. Stevens promised that in return for moving to reservations, the Indians would be cared for by the U.S. government. He lavished them with generalities and

Pioneers flocked to the frontier, traveling the Oregon Trail by wagon train through the Rocky Mountains and across the Columbia River, looking for adventure, fortune, or simply a fresh start. Despite Indian Wars and perilous travel, 50,000 people made the trek from the Midwest to Oregon Territory between 1840 and 1869, increasing the white population in the Northwest from a few hundred to over 100,000.

vague promises, and he also hinted that if the Indians didn't agree, their land would be confiscated by force without compensation.

In the end the Indians acquiesced to the treaty, although not all were happy about giving up 60,000 square miles of territory in exchange for the reservations and some vague promises from the U.S. government. Indian uprisings continued for several more years, exacerbated by the arrival of miners who crawled over Indian territory in search of gold.

Kamiakin, after hearing reports of Indian women being raped by some miners, led one war party that killed a group of whites. Over the next few years, various tribes divided their loyalties, first joining up with Kamiakin, then siding with the whites, then professing neutrality, depending on their own assessments of their chances for victory or defeat and whatever new threats or promises were made to them by the American government. In 1858, the commander of Fort Walla Walla finally crushed the remnants of Indian resistance, tracking down the last holdouts fleeing along the Snake River. The next year, Congress ratified the treaties negotiated by Isaac Stevens.

All was quiet on the Indian front for the next decade as Indians either moved to their reservations or were assimilated into the new population. A number of Indians however, stayed on the river and continued to fish, and as long as no white person came along and claimed the land, they were ignored. One Indian named Smohalla, of the Walla Walla tribe, lived on the river, and as time went on, he developed a reputation as a prophet. He said he had journeyed to the land of the dead and now had returned to tell the Indians how to live, recounting stories of the old Indian religion. The people who followed him were called Dreamers. When the whites heard about him, they suspected him of inciting Indians to rebellion, and the government began to blame Smohalla for renegades who sometimes caused trouble for the settlers.

In 1872, Oregon's superintendent for Indian affairs noted that the Indians had a religion which

> taught a new God is coming to their rescue; that all the Indians who have died are to be resurrected; that as they will then be very numerous and powerful they will be able to conquer the whites, recover their lands, and live as free and unrestrained as their fathers lived.[21]

In 1873, the Indian agent called a council. Smohalla did not show up, and nothing was accomplished. The Indian commissioner in Washington, D.C., reported to President Grant,

> About 2000 Indians are roaming on the Columbia River under the leadership of a self-constituted priest, Smohalla by name. He has inspired in his adherents veneration toward himself, and by his teaching superstition is fostered, unbridled license is

granted to passion, civilization is despised, and reservation Indians are looked upon with contempt and disdain. These Indians, in their present unsettled and unrestricted life, have no earthly mission beyond that of annoyance to settlers and hindrance to the opening of the country, and are a positive detriment to all other Indians.[22]

When the U.S. government decided to move some Nez Percé out of their reservation and send them to Lapwai in Idaho, their chief objected. The commander of the Military Department of the Columbia, General Oliver Otis Howard, decided the problem was caused by their belief in the Dreamer religion. General Howard met with Smohalla, who insisted that his people would never leave. Howard responded by calling another council, held at Lapwai in 1877.

A number of Dreamer priests showed up and talked for days about how the white man had no authority to take their land. General Howard responded by throwing one of the priests in prison. He then left to hunt down the still-protesting Nez Percé, who fled east into Idaho and eventually into Montana, on a thousand-mile trek to nowhere. In October 1877, government forces finally caught up with the holdouts and captured 400 Indians, mostly women and children because most of the men had already been killed.

After the Nez Percé War of 1877, these prisoners were shipped to a reservation in Oklahoma, where a third of them died in the sweltering heat. Eventually, the survivors were permitted to come back to the Northwest, now assigned not to the Nez Percé reservation at Lapwai but to another reservation in Washington, where they received a mixed reception. In the meantime, a warrant was issued for Smohalla's arrest, and on his own accord, he finally did what he vowed he never would: He took refuge on a reservation, where federal agents would leave him alone.

5

Development
of the River

By the early 1840s, with settlers streaming into Oregon, Fort Vancouver still stood as the center of commerce for the Columbia River, and Oregon City, located a few miles up the Willamette, offered a gathering place for Americans. Soon, two New Englanders staked a land claim on the banks of the Willamette, near the Columbia. They hired a crew to chop down the trees and laid out a plan for a few streets. Then the two men, Asa Lovejoy of Massachusetts and Francis Pettygrove of Maine, flipped a coin to decide who would get to name their new town. Pettygrove won the toss and bestowed the name of Portland on their little clearing, naming it after the largest city in his home state. But for the toss of this coin, the biggest city now on the Columbia would be named Boston.

Sea captain John H. Couch set the course for the future of Portland when he declared, "To this very point, I can bring any ship that can get into the mouth of the Columbia. And not a rod further."[23] Although his statement was not quite true, it was good enough for Couch's fellow captains. Couch retired to Portland, staking out a claim next to the property of Lovejoy and Pettygrove. Soon his friends were sailing their ships to Portland and nowhere else.

The produce of the Willamette Valley needed to get out, and the Columbia River was the only way until the railroads came. Before long, a road—the Great Plank Road—was built into Portland and farmers were taking their wares to Portland rather than to Oregon City. In 1849, the U.S. Post Office approved a Portland post office—Astoria was the other Oregon city with postal service—and a few years later, Portland was designated the terminus of the mail boat that sailed around Cape Horn from the East Coast.

Portland came into its own as a city because of an event that occurred 800 miles to the south, near Sacramento, California. A fellow by the name of James Marshall had journeyed to the Columbia River, but after a year, he drifted south to California, where he joined forces with Captain John Sutter, who had also gone to California by way of Oregon. Together they built a sawmill, and while working there in January 1848, Marshall discovered gold.

By the following year, the California gold rush was on. Men from Oregon mounted their horses and rode up the Willamette, then over the hills of southern Oregon and northern California, down into the Sacramento valley. A few people got rich on gold, but many more, including Oregonians who shipped grain, fruit, eggs, and lumber to California, saw opportunity in supplying the miners. Douglas firs were being cut down to build the wharfs of Portland, and ships were docking there to load cargo. Apples from Oregon went for more than $100 a bushel in San Francisco. Eggs sold for a dollar a piece in the gold mines.

Portland became the transportation hub of the Northwest. Although the Hudson's Bay Company had intermittently run a small steamship from Fort Vancouver to the Pacific and up and down the Willamette, the first American steamship crossed the Columbia Bar in 1850 and soon began running a regular route between Portland and Astoria. A few years later, a steamboat was brought to Oregon in several pieces and assembled above the Cascades, where it plied the inland routes.

By the mid-1850s, a person could travel by steamer from Astoria to the Snake River, changing boats three times: once in Portland, again at the Cascades, and again at The Dalles. By 1860, the boat owners and the portage road owners had formed the Oregon Steam Navigation Company (OSN), which monopolized transportation on the Columbia for years. The OSN started with six boats in the river below the Cascades, four that operated from the Cascades to The Dalles, and one that ran above Celilo Falls, just upriver from The Dalles.

The first passengers were miners spreading out from California in search of more gold. As miner traffic died off, the OSN made its money on freight and farm goods. The company expanded quickly, buying up competing boats and taking control of the portage roads around the rapids, replacing wagons and mules with short steam railroad lines.

Passengers would board a steamer in Portland, which would

Portland, Oregon, located on the Willamette River, a tributary of the Columbia, was founded in the 1840s by Asa Lovejoy and Francis Pettygrove. During the Gold Rush, Portland came into its own as the transportation hub of the Northwest, and by the turn of the twentieth century it was a prosperous city with booming logging, fishing, and shipping industries.

take them 65 miles to the Cascades, and then would get off and ride a five-mile rail line around the rapids. Then they would board a second boat for another 50 miles, which would take them out of the humid, timbered western slope of Oregon and into the dry, breezy territory east of the mountains. Reaching The Dalles, passengers would then mount another rail and ride 14 more miles above Celilo Falls, where yet another steamer could take him as far as Lewiston, Idaho, 280 miles farther up the Snake River. The ride upriver from Portland to Lewiston took two to three days. The ride down, with the current, was a one-day affair.

The trip aboard a riverboat was not always smooth. The wind could howl through the canyons, and waves could easily rise to five feet. Dust storms sometimes blew off the silty soil of eastern Washington, making visibility poor along the river. Accidents were not unheard-of. In 1858, one steamship cast off above the Cascades before getting up a head of steam. Without power, it drifted down the current through the rapids of the Cascades stern first, finally banging against a rock. The boat survived, but one passenger was killed when he panicked and jumped overboard.

One boat on the Willamette blew up, killing 28 people. In 1887, a fire broke out aboard a steamship as it was nearing Astoria. The captain rammed the boat onto a sandbar, so the passengers were able to jump off into shallow water, where they wouldn't drown. The ship suffered only one casualty: a man passed out drunk in his cabin.

With gold fever in the air, adventuresome men continued to scour the mountain streams of the Columbia system for precious metals. Some deposits were found in Canada, drawing men up north. Larger discoveries were made along the Clearwater River in 1860, and soon miners were racing to Idaho. Close behind them went the ranchers and cowboys, driving their cattle into pasturelands along the Walla Walla, Umatilla, and Yakima Rivers.

Within a year, more than $1 million in gold was found in Idaho, and these riches brought more people to service the mining camps. Farmers found fields along various Columbia tributaries that would support wheat, corn, and barley, as well as apple orchards. Cattlemen drove more herds upriver. Traders accompanied them all, ready to profit from the miners' appetites for food, clothes, and provisions. Early twentieth-century historian William Lyman noted, "A considerable part of these goods, we regret to narrate, consisted of material for spirituous refreshments." [24]

Until the railroads were built along the river, farmers would bring their goods to the river to load them on the steamboats. In some places, where the river wended through bluffs sometimes 1,000 to 2,000 feet high, farmers built chutes to transport their grain down to the river. At first, the grain traveled so fast down the chutes that it was scorched by friction. The farmers crafted baffles, or upturns, in the chutes to slow down the grain, and the system worked well enough to continue to serve farmers into the twentieth century.

By the 1860s, there was a wide network of railroads in the East, but not until after the Civil War could the nation focus on expanding railroads west of the Mississippi. A railroad act signed by President Lincoln offered free land, as well as cash subsidies, to the Central and the Union Pacific for building a transcontinental railroad. The last spike was pounded in 1869, finally linking San Francisco to the East Coast.

On the Columbia River, railroads began as short trunk lines to ease portages around sections of the river that could not be navigated. Then lines expanded out from the river to haul wheat and other crops to the riverbank. As soon as the transcontinental railroad was completed, Portland entrepreneurs started laying track down the Willamette to connect with the California line. When this effort collapsed because of a lack of money, railroad pioneer Henry Villard bought out the company and completed the rail link to California. Villard also bought the OSN and reorganized it as the Oregon Railway & Navigation Company, expanding his rail monopoly to steamships.

Meanwhile, officials in Washington had passed an act to build another transcontinental railroad from the Great Lakes to the Northwest to be called the Northern Pacific. The act offered even more land than the one authorizing the San Francisco line but no cash, so the Northern Pacific was strapped for money from the start. After going into bankruptcy in 1873, with tracks laid only as far west as Bismarck, North Dakota, this company, too, was gobbled up by Henry Villard. With the help of imported Chinese and Irish laborers, he finished building the rail link to Portland in 1883 and to Seattle in 1887.

James J. Hill, a railroad tycoon from Minnesota, built a second railroad to the Northwest a few years later. The Great Northern completed a link to Seattle by way of Spokane, which by then was developing as the lumber and wheat capital of eastern Washington. These two transcontinental railroads, along with an expanding system throughout the Northwest, brought Northwest timber and farm produce to Midwest and California markets and carried yet more newcomers to the Columbia River, where they would prosper by farming and fishing and cutting down trees.

Meanwhile, above the 49th parallel, the Canadians were building their own transcontinental railroad. In November 1885, workers laid the last section of track and the link between Montreal and Vancouver was completed. The Canadian Pacific Railway (CPR) crossed the Columbia in two places: at Golden in the east, where the river ran north, and again at Revelstoke, farther west, where the river ran south. Although the CPR brought money and workers to the Upper Columbia, the terrain in this wild part of the river was too rough for the kind of expansive development taking place nearer the coast.

Still, a makeshift system of steamboats ran up and down the Upper Columbia. One intrepid entrepreneur, a European hunter and world traveler named William Adolph Baillie-Graham, even dug a canal to connect the headwaters of the Columbia with the Kootenay River, across Canal Flats. This canal was completed in 1889. It was 6,700 feet long and 45 feet wide and equipped with one 100-by-35-foot lock. At least one steamboat made the crossing, but the canal never came close to being a commercial success. The town of Canal Flats never developed into anything more than a few buildings, and eventually Baille-Graham returned to Europe a poorer but wiser man.

Though these early efforts to tame the wild river were halting, the appetite for exploiting the resources of the river knew no bounds. Methods for preserving foods by canning had been discovered in the 1800s, and in 1867, a cannery was assembled on the shores of the Lower Columbia. Fishing the river was nothing new, but early efforts were restricted by the inability to

THE HOUSE WHERE NO ONE LIVED

Today, about a hundred miles east of Portland, perched 900 feet above the Columbia River on a windswept bluff, stands the Maryhill Museum of Art. The museum's collection includes American paintings and Native American handiwork. It also features the royal regalia of Queen Marie of Romania, including her coronation gown, as well as a number of Russian religious icons.

Why is there Eastern European artwork in a museum of the Northwest? It goes back to the man who built this three-story castle of concrete and stone. A native of North Carolina, Sam Hill graduated from Harvard in 1879 and went to work for the great railroader Jim Hill, no relation to him. In 1888, Sam Hill married the boss's oldest daughter, Mary Hill, and the young man proved enormously successful in business. He helped expand the Great Northern Railway throughout the Northwest. He became an overseer of Harvard University and traveled the world and became friends with kings and princes.

On one of his extended visits to the Northwest, Sam Hill bought 7,000 acres of barren land on the north bank of the Columbia River in Washington's Klickitat County. Sam Hill began to build his castle, which he named Maryhill from the start. Although Mary Hill was his wife, she never went near the place and never even saw the building. Instead, Sam Hill said the castle would be a retreat for Quakers, or a school for farmers, or perhaps even a library.

One day in 1926, when the castle was almost finished, Hill announced that one of his friends, Queen Marie of Romania—granddaughter of both Queen Victoria of England and Czar Alexander II of Russia—would dedicate the building. She arrived by way of Portland, bearing 15 crates of artifacts and artwork for what was now to be a museum.

Sam Hill, son-in-law of a great railroad builder, was a builder of another sort. He championed the development of highways throughout Washington and Oregon, and even before the end of his life, these roads began to eclipse the railroad as a means of transportation. Many of the smaller logging railroads lost business to trucks, and the rails were pulled up. Sam Hill died in 1931, and his ashes were placed on a bluff overlooking the Columbia a few miles from Maryhill.

preserve fish for export. Fishing by Indians and white settlers therefore was done largely for local consumption.

Now the harvesting of fish began in earnest. By 1876, more than 20 million pounds of fish, chiefly salmon, were caught in the Lower Columbia River and canned. Only the depletion of salmon in the twentieth century slowed the Columbia fishing industry. Fishermen used boats, traps, nets, fish wheels, and anything else to reel ashore the catch. Fish wheels were waterwheels placed in narrow swift channels, with wire buckets attached along the wheels to haul in the fish. Another effective method was playing out a big fish net into the channel and then using horses on shore to pull the net together and trap the fish.

When fishing was slow, many fishermen turned to logging. In the 1800s, huge Douglas firs grew along the river from the Pacific as far inland as the Cascades. At first, logging was done simply to clear the land. Portland was known as Stump Town in its early days because the trees were cut a few feet off the ground to make way for the buildings. The stumps were painted white so they could be seen at night.

The Hudson's Bay Company had a water-powered sawmill near Fort Vancouver as early as the 1820s to supply boards for building the stockade. Several mills popped up along the river in the first half of the century to provide lumber for the local housing market and later for the boilers of steamboats. Commercial logging for export did not get underway until the California gold rush brought demand for wood to build San Francisco. The first steam sawmill in the Northwest began puffing away in Portland in 1850, and then the exporting of lumber began in earnest.

In the beginning, Douglas firs were cut along the river; then the limbs were sliced off and the logs were rolled into the river and floated to the nearest sawmill. After the shores of the river were cut bare and logging retreated up the hills, loggers built skid roads to move the felled trees to the river. Men would clear a path from the riverbank into the forest. Then, at suitable intervals, they would lay trees across the path, sinking them halfway into the muddy ground. These were the skids, which provided a track to prevent the logs from hanging up in the mud and underbrush. Loggers then hitched steers to the big logs and, guided by the curses of a bullwhacker, the animals would pull the logs over the tracks to the river.

As the logging moved back from the river, clever lumbermen employed the tributaries of the Columbia to move the wood. They would dam up a river, stockpile logs all summer and fall, and in the spring, when the river was at flood stage, they would destroy the dam and wash the wood down to the Columbia.

East of the Cascades, smaller trees grew—not the big Douglas firs, but ponderosa pine, white pine, and spruce—up in Idaho and British Columbia. Interest in these forests grew as the railroads came in from the east. Logs were brought to the mills in the usual way—by rail, water, or animal power—then they were cut into boards that were shipped east by railroad to build the cities and towns of the Midwest.

Skid Road became a well-known section of the typical Northwestern town. The name itself came from Seattle, where initially a skid road brought logs right to the downtown waterfront. Saloons, flophouses, cheap hotels, and employment offices grew up around Seattle's skid road. Before long, this district in Seattle, and in every other town in the Northwest, was known as Skid Road—sometimes called Skid Row—the place where loggers, miners, fishermen, and other itinerant workers gravitated when they wanted to blow off steam.

Spokane's Skid Road boasted a saloon called Jimmy Durkin's. The saloon had a safe where many a logger from the pine camps squirreled away his money. For those who had spent all their money, Jimmy Durkin's was a place to get a loan. In a nod to family values, above the bar was a sign: "If Children Need Shoes, Don't Buy Booze."[25]

Loggers, fishermen, miners, seamen—they were all a rough bunch of people. They worked hard and often had no families, and they lived raucous lives. Plenty of bars and other nightspots dotted every Northwest town to keep them entertained. The Workingman's Club in Portland, which took up most of a city block, offered organ music, free lunch and reportedly, at 684 feet, the longest bar in the world.

Portland's Skid Road boasted dozens of nightspots for the loggers, along with a number of boardinghouses where loggers and sailors and fishermen could sleep off their weekend indiscretions. The boardinghouses could be dangerous places. Men were known to be kidnapped by "crimps"—brokers who were paid to provide labor for the ships coming in and out of Portland. The most famous crimp, Bunco Kelly, boasted of having sent over a thousand landlubbers, as well as twice as many legitimate sailors, out to sea. He would drug his prospects, carry them on board a ship, and collect a finder's fee from the captain. It's said that Kelly once delivered a wooden Indian taken from the front of a cigar store to a British ship. "He's awful drunk," he told the captain as he collected his fee, "but he'll make you a prime hand." [26]

Bunco Kelly was finally sent away to prison for murder, and eventually the Skid Road of Portland and other river cities declined as the Northwest became more settled. Workers got married and had families. They moved into their own homes instead of living in logging camps, and labor unions grew up in the twentieth century to protect their jobs, offer them some measure of on-the-job safety, and serve as an employment agency when times got tough.

6

Dam It Up

The soil in eastern Washington was rich but dry. In the few places where farmers constructed small irrigation ditches, they enjoyed a bountiful harvest. If only there was some way to get water from the big river, the land would blossom.

In 1917, a lawyer named Billy Clapp came up with the idea of building a big dam across the Columbia River near his home in Ephrata, Washington. The dam would create a lake reaching as far north as the Canadian border, and he envisioned the water spilling over into Grand Coulee to create a big reservoir. The water could then be filtered southward to irrigate the fertile but dry land of the Columbia Basin—where Billy Clapp's town of Ephrata happened to be located. Meanwhile, water rushing over the dam could turn turbines that would produce an almost infinite amount of cheap electricity.

Billy Clapp knew as well as anyone that when settlers first arrived in eastern Washington they found the land easy to plow. Plenty of crops sprung from that rich soil left behind by the Ice Age. But after a few years, with the region's sparse rainfall, the fields began to fail. By the early 1900s, people who had arrived with the railroads 20 and 30 years before were abandoning their farms and moving away.

The notion of improving and harnessing the Columbia River was not a new one. In 1896, a 3,000-foot-long canal, called the Cascades Locks, had been completed around the rapids to give passenger boats and freighters safe passage around the dangerous waters. Now, instead of getting off one boat, taking a stage or a railroad around the rapids, and boarding another boat, people—and cargo as well—could ride the river nonstop.

In 1915, the United States Army Corps of Engineers completed another, longer canal-and-lock system around Celilo Falls. And at the mouth of the river, engineers had dredged the channel and built long jetties out into the ocean. More than 8 million tons of automobile-size boulders had been hauled to the ocean by train to create a jetty that in some places was taller than a five-story building. The project protected the entrance to the Columbia and helped prevent sand and silt from choking the channel. By 1900, the Columbia Bar was no longer the dangerous problem it had presented to early settlers.

Billy Clapp's idea was more ambitious by far. Dubbed the Columbia Basin Project, the visionary proposal was given a boost the following year when Rufus Woods, editor and publisher of the *Wenatchee World,* wrote a number of articles supporting the idea. Others liked the project because it would give a big boost to the local economy. Eventually, Franklin D. Roosevelt, campaigning for vice president in 1920, caught wind of the proposal and threw his support behind the idea of a dam. The Democratic presidential platform that year included a provision for the development of the Columbia River to produce cheap water and electricity for farmers and small businessmen in the Northwest.

Roosevelt lost the 1920 election, and soon the economic boom of the 1920s took hold, focusing attention on Wall Street and big business rather than on helping rural people in this still-remote corner of the country. The idea for a big federal dam was lost in the noise of the Roaring 20s—but it didn't go away.

Meanwhile, a private concern, the Puget Sound Light & Power Company, purchased land below the Wenatchee River at a stretch of water called Rock Island Rapids. The company wanted to build a relatively low and modest dam to produce electricity for its growing base of customers. The property was adjacent to the Northern Pacific Railroad, so construction supplies could be brought in easily. Work began in January 1930. The 3,800-foot-long Rock Island Dam, with four power generators, was completed in 1933. It was the first dam to span the Columbia and today is the oldest and smallest dam on the river.

The Depression of the 1930s followed the boom of the 1920s, and Franklin Roosevelt was elected president in 1932.

The construction of the Grand Coulee Dam on the Columbia River was one of many public projects approved by President Franklin D. Roosevelt in hopes of revitalizing the U.S. economy during the Depression. Supporters of the dam promised the construction of the enormous structure, completed in 1942, would provide jobs, cheap electricity, and improved irrigation and navigation. The power generated by the dam was essential during World War II, supporting the production of aluminum for airplanes and ships built in the region.

Roosevelt had a big appetite for large public projects as a way to get the economy moving again, and out of Washington, D.C., the Army Corps of Engineers launched an overall survey of American rivers. Among the conclusions was that the federal government should build dams along the Columbia

River to improve navigation, generate electricity, and provide irrigation.

Three months after he was inaugurated, Roosevelt authorized both the Grand Coulee Dam and the Bonneville Dam, a smaller structure to be built at the lower Cascades. The following year, 1934, Roosevelt returned to the Columbia. He compared the river to the Hudson River, along which he had grown up, noting that the Hudson had became the first gateway to the west with the building of the Erie Canal in the early 1800s. The president envisioned the Columbia as the Hudson of the West Coast. Once a series of dams and locks was constructed along the river, the Columbia would open the Northwest, offering modern navigation and life-giving irrigation to a broad range of desert scrubland.

Private utility companies like Puget Sound, fearing encroachment from the government on their profitable monopolies, opposed the federal dams. They charged that government dam building was socialistic. Some called supporters of the dam "coulee communists." One critic, a New York congressman, scoffed at the dam at Grand Coulee: "All this dam would do is provide water for thirsty jackrabbits and for light bulbs in Indian tepees."[27] Supporters claimed that the dam would be a windfall for average people. One farmer told Richard Neuberger, a Portland-born journalist in New York, "That river belongs to us, not Wall Street."[28]

Work began in 1933 on the Bonneville Dam, located 190 miles upriver from the Pacific. It was named after Captain Benjamin Bonneville, the adventurer made famous by Washington Irving. The dam was completed in 1938, and the giant turbines began churning out power.

The dam backed up the river for miles, flooding the Cascades Locks and the great chute of the Columbia that so troubled the immigrants who arrived along the last leg of the Oregon Trail. The dam featured a spillway to regulate the height of the water in the reservoir behind it, a powerhouse to produce electricity, a lock to transport vessels above and below the dam, and three "fish ways" allowing salmon to swim around the dam.

Once Roosevelt approved these projects, word spread throughout the nation, especially across the drought-plagued Midwest farm belt, that paying jobs were available in Washington. The unemployed from around the country poured in. In 1932, there were six people living at Grand Coulee. By 1934, 7,000 men and a handful of women had crowded into the area.

In 1937, when the Grand Coulee Dam was half-finished, President Roosevelt returned and pronounced Grand Coulee the largest structure ever built by man. He was not quite accurate—the Great Wall of China was bigger—but it was indeed an ambitious undertaking. More than 5,000 workers would take almost 10 years to build the massive structure. When completed, the Grand Coulee Dam would stretch almost a mile wide. Concrete was sunk down to bedrock, 200 feet below the surface of the river in some places. In all, the dam is 550 feet tall and contains enough concrete to build a highway around the perimeter of the United States.

The dam would back up the Columbia River 150 miles to the Canadian border, forming a long, slender body of water named Franklin D. Roosevelt Lake. The lake drowned Kettle Falls, the ancient Indian fishing spot, as well as a number of towns along the river that were either abandoned or else moved to higher ground.

"We look forward not only to the great good this will do in the development of power but also in the development of thousands of homes, the bringing in of millions of acres of new land for future Americans," said Roosevelt.[29] Indeed, thousands more victims of the Depression did flow into Washington and Oregon from the Midwest, looking for a small piece of land to support their families.

In 1937, J.D. Ross, head of Seattle City Light, was put in charge of the newly created Bonneville Power Administration (BPA), the agency set up to control and distribute power generated by the Columbia River dams. As expected, Ross set low rates for electricity. Residents of the area could light their homes for only $1 a month. Their total electric bill, including heat, averaged $7.50 per month.

The BPA also hired a publicity director, Stephen Kahn, whose mission was to promote the development of the Columbia River. He in turn hired a film director to make a documentary called *Hydro!,* an inspirational film celebrating the Columbia River dams. He signed folksinger Woody Guthrie to write songs about the river and the migrant farmers who would work the irrigated land. Guthrie's most famous song was "Roll On, Columbia":

> And on up the river at Grand Coulee Dam
> The mightiest thing every built by a man
> To run the great factories for Old Uncle Sam,
> It's roll on, Columbia, roll on.[30]

Records indicate that 80 men died building the Grand Coulee Dam. Stories relate how men fell into the structure and were buried alive in the drying concrete, although official documents claim that there are no bodies built into the dam. Other rumors said that engineers found gold when they were digging to lay the base of the dam.

The Grand Coulee was officially opened in 1942 when a Nez Percé chief from nearby Colville Reservation threw the switch and power started throbbing from the monstrous mountain of concrete. Although no one could know what all that power would be used for when the project was started, by the time the dam was completed World War II had burst on the nation. Four million people migrated to the West Coast during the war to find work in expanding industries. Most of the Grand Coulee electricity went to making aluminum for the war effort: the aluminum exteriors for airplanes assembled by Boeing and the aluminum plates for ships built in the Portland and Vancouver shipyards.

MYSTERIOUS PASSENGER

The Northwest has had its share of eccentric characters but none more so than D.B. Cooper. On November 24, 1971, a man who identified himself as Dan Cooper boarded a Northwest Airlines 727 bound from Portland to Seattle. Sitting toward the back of the half-empty plane, he passed a note to a flight attendant demanding four parachutes and $200,000 in unmarked bills. "No funny stuff,"* the note said, and also mentioned that Cooper had a bomb. He opened a briefcase, revealing some red cylinders and wires.

The plane circled Seattle airport until the FBI reported that the parachutes and money were ready. Then the captain landed. Cooper allowed passengers to deplane, and the money and parachutes were brought on board. Then Cooper demanded that the plane take off for Mexico, flying at no more than 170 mph. and lower than 10,000 feet.

The plane departed at 7:44 P.M. A few minutes later, Cooper told the flight attendant to go up to the cockpit. Just as she shut the curtain to the first-class cabin she saw Cooper tying something around his waist—presumably the bag of money. At 8:00 P.M., the pilot saw the red warning light come on, indicating that a door was open. He asked over the intercom, "Is everything okay back there? Is there anything we can do for you?" The answer was "No!"** That was the last anyone heard from D.B. Cooper.

The U.S. Air Force had sent a jet to tail the Northwest plane, and the FBI attempted to follow in a helicopter. In the darkness, no one could see where or when Cooper jumped. The FBI attempted to locate Cooper on the ground, but their efforts were hampered by darkness and bad weather. About 300 people searched for more than a month, but no sign of Cooper or the money was found.

Almost 10 years later, on February 10, 1980, a boy digging along the shore of the Columbia, northwest of Vancouver, found $5,800 in badly deteriorated $20 bills, along with some broken rubber bands. The FBI matched these bills to

Construction of the Grand Coulee ushered in a great era of dam building along the Columbia that led to a taming of the wild river of the West. The rough-running river of David Thompson, Marcus Whitman, and John McLoughlin became a series of long slender lakes, one after another, from Bonneville up into Canada—which built three of its own dams after a 1964 the serial numbers of the bills given to D.B. Cooper. No other signs of D.B. Cooper were ever found.

The FBI speculates that D.B. Cooper probably died either during his descent or shortly afterward. Jumping into the night, he would not know where he was landing. He might have dropped in the river. The weather was cold and stormy, and he had no food and no way to keep warm. It was unlikely that he had a plan to rendezvous with an accomplice, because he did not instruct the pilot to fly a specific course—so he could only guess at the location of his drop zone.

A Portland man named Daniel B. Cooper was questioned about the crime and exonerated. Some say that copycat Richard Floyd McCoy, who hijacked a 727 in 1972, was the real D.B. Cooper. No one knows for sure, though, because he was shot and killed trying to escape capture in 1974. In August 2000, a Florida woman reported that her husband confessed on his deathbed that he was D.B. Cooper. The man resembled FBI sketches of Cooper, and he had spent some time in prison. After an investigation, the FBI was unable to either discount or prove the account. In all, more than 1,000 suspects have been investigated for the crime, and to this day people still call the F.B.I. claiming that their husband or ex-boyfriend is the real D.B. Cooper.

Although D.B. Cooper himself is probably dead, his legend lives on: A movie was made about him starring Robert Duvall, there is a restaurant, and T-shirts and posters have been sold. Every year, Ariel, Washington, a town near the spot where Cooper jumped, hosts a D.B. Cooper festival during the week of Thanksgiving.

* Quoted in *super70s.com*, "Disappearance of D.B. Cooper"

** Quoted in *super70s.com*, "Disappearance of D.B. Cooper," also in Richard Seven, "D.B. Cooper," *seattletimes.com*, via *who2.com/dbcooper.html*

treaty provided American investment in return for subsidized electric prices.

Today, the Columbia Basin Project irrigates an area the size of Rhode Island, about 640,000 acres. Half the land originally intended for irrigation has never been watered, because support for the spread of irrigation began to wither. Nobody

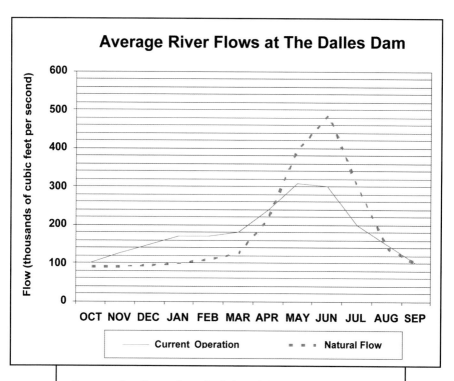

Average River Flows at The Dalles Dam

Flow (thousands of cubic feet per second)

OCT NOV DEC JAN FEB MAR APR MAY JUN JUL AUG SEP

——— Current Operation   - - - Natural Flow

Dam construction and manipulation of the river were essential to the prosperity of the Columbia River Northwest, but their effects were not entirely positive. The human activity along the river pushed out wildlife and trees, with factories and nuclear sites polluting the area. Most significantly, the once fast and clear river now flows slack and dirty, creating an inhospitable environment for the salmon and other fish that once were caught by the ton. [Source: Northwest Power Planning Council. Fourth Northwest Power Plan, Portland OR, 1996, p. 4–5]

thought about the real cost of all that cheap power and irrigation during the 1930s—people were just trying to survive the Depression—and in the 1940s, all worries focused on winning the war.

As fishermen's nets came up empty, people eventually noticed that the salmon were disappearing from the river. Water that once ran free and clear was now slack and dirty, like a stopped-up bathtub. Indians who once prospered along the river were now wasting their lives cooped up on reservations or else in prison. The Douglas fir and other native trees that once lined the banks of the Columbia had been replaced by a string of federal Superfund sites that marked the waste from pulp mills, smelters, canneries, and the largest nuclear waste dump within a thousand miles.

In 1992, the American Rivers Council, an environmental group, cited the Columbia as the most endangered river in the United States. The river had been used, for sure, but had it been used up?

7

The Promise Fulfilled

In late 1942, government officials came to one section of the Columbia River near the Tri-Cities of Pasco, Kennewick, and Richland and quietly began to ask questions. Satisfied that this area, above where the Snake meets the Columbia, had plenty of water and abundant electricity, the feds acquired almost half a million acres of scrubland the next year. They began to build some sort of secret project at a place called Hanford.

A number of residents, about 1,200 of them, were moved out of the area, and a huge contingent of engineers, scientists, and workers crowded onto the site, living in tents and makeshift government housing. The new workers didn't talk much about why they were there—it turned out that a lot of those workers didn't *know* why they were there—and the government pressured newspapers not to publicize the project.

When World War II was over and two atomic bombs had been dropped on Japan, people finally learned what was going on. "IT'S ATOMIC BOMBS," read the big headline of a Hanford newspaper.[31] The Hanford Atomic Engineering Project had been producing the plutonium used in nuclear bombs. Eight reactors rose up next to the Columbia River. The water rumbling down from the Rockies was being pumped into Hanford to cool the radioactive material developed there.

After World War II, the Hanford site proved useful for the next contest: the Cold War. Scientists produced 53 tons of plutonium inside those atomic reactors, turning uranium into the fuel for the U.S. nuclear arsenal. Meanwhile, the city of Richland sported the Atomic Bowling Lanes and offered the Atomic TV repair shop. Football players at the high school had a mushroom-shaped cloud on their helmets and were known as the Bombers.

In the 1970s, the Washington Public Power Supply System (WPPSS) also started to build several nuclear power plants at the Hanford site. However, public pressure in the wake of

From the time settlers first arrived in the Northwest, they exploited the Columbia River region, leveling trees, over-fishing, eliminating wildlife and Native Americans, and eventually building dams and power plants which altered the river's natural flow. Today, this 50-mile stretch of the Columbia along the former Hanford nuclear plant site is the only section of the river that resembles its appearance in the 1800s.

the nuclear accident at Pennsylvania's Three Mile Island plant caused WPPSS to close down its nuclear operations. The agency defaulted on its bonds in 1983—it became known as WHOOPS—and caused the kind of financial problems that brought about 60 lawsuits, resulted in dramatically higher electricity rates throughout the Northwest, and undermined the credibility of federal administration of the river.

Today, with the Cold War over, all Hanford reactors are closed down. The focus of attention is no longer on building bombs or generating electricity but on cleaning up radioactive waste. Federal agencies constantly test the water in the Columbia, as well as any dead animals found in the area, to make sure no pollution is leaking out from the nuclear site. The Tri-Cities area of Washington, which built its prosperity on the making of nuclear bombs, now owes its livelihood to environmental containment and cleanup of nuclear waste.

Ironically, the 50-mile stretch of the Columbia along the Hanford Reach is now the most natural and wild part of the river that exists below the Canadian border. A dam here would flood the contaminated soil around Hanford and risk leaking nuclear waste into the river. Hanford therefore is one of the few places above Bonneville Dam where the river looks like it did back in the 1800s and for thousands of years before that. Deer and elk, bobcats and badgers, birds and waterfowl all thrive in the area.

Unfortunately, Native Americans have not been as lucky as the wildlife. In 1960, The Dalles Dam flooded the last of the great fishing spots, Celilo Falls, where Indians had been catching salmon for thousands of years. For the loss of the site, the U.S. government paid the tribes $26.8 million. By this time, Northwest Indians had sold or otherwise lost two-thirds of the reservation land originally ceded to them in the treaty arranged by Washington territorial governor Isaac Stevens.

The 1855 treaty did promise that the Indians could continue to fish in the Columbia River at their usual and accustomed fishing grounds, in common with other citizens of Washington, so some Indians continued to find spots to fish along the river, although their share of the total salmon catch was down to about 1 percent. The government discouraged them, harassed them, and fined them but never was too serious about enforcement. White commercial fishing interests didn't like it, and sport fishermen felt that Indians were getting preferential treatment. In 1966, the Oregon State Fish Commission announced it would enforce its restrictive regulations on the Indians. Some of the Indians created their own fishing commission, which declared a season that started earlier than the state season. Again the Indians fished, and they were ticketed and fined, and often the fines were suspended. In 1968, one group of Native Americans decided to press the issue.

David Sohappy, a U.S. Army veteran who also happened to be a distant relation of Smohalla, the late nineteenth-century prophet who inspired the Dreamer religion, went fishing with his nephew. The two men were arrested by Washington officials, given 30-day suspended sentences, and fined $50. David appealed the case to the state superior court, asking that the salmon seasons set by the states of Oregon and Washington be declared invalid because they violated treaty rights. The case became known as *Sohappy* v. *Smith*.

In October 1969, U.S. district court judge Robert Belloni ruled that the states could not restrict Indian fishing rights, except in cases in which there were clear conservation issues. He decided that the rights of the Indians were more important than state law. The judge also declared that the Indians should get a fair and equitable share of the fish as outlined in the original treaties from the 1850s.

This ruling was later interpreted to mean that Native Americans should get half the catch from the river—even though they now represented less than 2 percent of the population—and Indians would be allowed an even greater amount if the extra fish were not sold but were either eaten by the Indians themselves or else used in religious ceremonies. Naturally, white fishing interests, viewing Native Americans as just one more special interest group lobbying for more than their fair share, were outraged at the decision. Resentment grew as salmon runs continued to decline throughout the 1970s.

Tensions simmered among white commercial fishermen,

white sport fishermen, and the Native Americans over how much fish they were each allowed to catch. Then, in 1981, a federal bill sponsored by Washington Senator Slade Gorton was passed into law as part of the Lacey Act. The law made it a federal crime for anyone to violate fishing regulations and changed illegal fishing from a misdemeanor to a felony.

Agents for the National Marine Fisheries Service, a division of the U.S. Department of Commerce, set up a sting operation to purchase fish from the Sohappys and their fellow Indians, who were catching fish for sale instead of their own personal use. The project was called "Salmonscam," and a flurry of indictments followed. Prosecutors charged that the Indians were exploiting their own traditions for profit and over-fishing the waters of the Columbia in the process. Defenders of the Indians claimed that they were fishing in accordance with their traditions and their culture and within their agreed-upon treaty rights.

Seventy people were arrested and 19 indicted. They were found innocent of conspiracy charges, but 13 people were guilty of illegal fish sales. Most of the Indians were put on probation; some received fines. Several were sentenced to prison, including David Sohappy, who was found guilty on four felony counts, which included selling 4,300 pounds of fish. His son was also convicted and sentenced to five years in prison for selling 313 pounds of fish.

Ten years of controversy, appeals, and political maneuvering followed, but in the end several fishermen, including the two Sohappys, spent a number of months in federal prison. Nothing was finally resolved about who could fish for what in the river. All that was certain was that the number of fish in the Columbia River were fewer and fewer—and Native Americans were catching less and less of what was left.

Today, the Columbia River is known as much for tourism as it is for fishing, irrigation, or electric-power generation. Visitors flock to view the Grand Coulee Dam, where during

THE LEGACY OF LONESOME LARRY

In 1900, before the dams were built, over 40 million pounds of fish were caught in the Columbia. By 1980, the catch was down to 2 million. Since then, fishing seasons have been shortened, and in some cases eliminated, to try to save the few remaining fish.

Over the years, a number of trends along the river have conspired to kill the salmon. Farming and logging have damaged the streambeds of the Columbia system, stripping them of the food, shade, and hiding places salmon need to give birth to their young. Although fish ladders have been built into a number of Columbia River dams, the Grand Coulee was constructed with no ladders at all. Salmon once swam from the Pacific all the way to Columbia Lake at the source of the river. Now the upper half of the river has been lost to them.

Dams pose another problem for the salmon. After adult salmon swim upriver, lay their eggs, and die, the salmon who are born need to make it back to the ocean. The wild river used to give them a swift ride down to the Pacific. Now the water is slack, moving slowly behind the dams. Young salmon now expend much more energy making that return voyage, and when the fish arrive at the dams, they must run the gauntlet of the spillway or the power turbines. Each dam kills approximately 10 percent of the fish swimming through its mechanisms. For schools of salmon negotiating five or six dams, half are killed. In fact, estimates say that only about 1 percent of the salmon make it down the river to the Pacific and then return, fighting their way back up the Columbia to spawn.

the summer there are daily guided tours and every night a laser light show plays against the massive face of the dam. There is a July 4th Festival, billed as "a patriotic tribute to old-fashioned family fun" complete with live bands and fireworks exploding off the top of the dam.

In July, the Tri-Cities area of Pasco, Kennewick, and Richland sponsors a hydroplane race, the Budweiser Columbia Cup, which lures 50,000 fans. Accompanying the race are a beauty contest, an air show, and a strongman competition.

In 1992, only one adult sockeye salmon survived the 900-mile swim up the Columbia and the Snake to spawn in Idaho's Redfish Lake. The fish was named Lonesome Larry, and Idaho's then-governor Cecil Andrus had him stuffed and mounted to demonstrate the perilous position of the salmon.

Scientists saved Lonesome Larry's sperm and froze it, using it to fertilize the eggs of female sockeye salmon who made it back to Idaho in subsequent years. This breeding program is just one of many that environmentalists are using to try to save the fish. No one knows how many of Lonesome Larry's descendents are swimming in the Columbia, but everyone agrees that there are precious few wild salmon left in the river. Instead, most are hatchery fish, raised by fish agencies in climate-controlled tanks along the river.

About 80 million hatchery fish are pumped into the Snake and Columbia Rivers every year. Although some people question the long-term viability of the program, because hatchery fish are not as hardy as their wild cousins, it has brought back the salmon count in recent years and saved the Washington and Oregon fishing industry.

In 2001, 2 million salmon were counted running through Bonneville Dam, the most since the dam was opened in 1937. The situation has improved enough for the second fishing season in 30 years to be opened in eastern Washington for the summer of 2003, with a daily limit of six salmon. For the first time in a long time, the Washington Department of Fish and Wildlife predicted a strong run. Let's hope they're right.

Several Columbia tributaries are known for their whitewater rafting expeditions. Class 3 and Class 4 rapids, for example, bubble down the Klickitat and White Salmon Rivers from Mount Adams to the Columbia. The Columbia Gorge, once the feared neck of the Columbia, has become known as a prized windsurfing site. "Board-heads" from around the world log more than 300,000 windsurfing days per year on this 40-mile stretch of the Columbia, known for its constantly blowing breezes. The town of Hood River,

Oregon, where the Hood meets the Columbia, has become a mecca for windsurfers, as well as headquarters for the Columbia Gorge Windsurfing Association.

The river that started out as a European dream for a passage to Asia now attracts tourists from Asia. There are also small Asian communities on the Columbia, legacies of laborers imported to work in the mines and on the railroads. The real significance of the Columbia turned out not to be as a passage through North American but an entranceway into North America, opening up the Northwest to settlement and development, all of which goes on to this day.

The Columbia River became a resource to feed the American appetite—first for furs, then for space and food and minerals and timber. Ironically, one of the last resources to be developed out of the Columbia was the water itself, which became a kind of religion in the Northwest for much of the twentieth century. The water irrigated eastern Oregon and Washington, allowing these areas to become some of the richest farmland in the United States. If you've ever eaten a Red Delicious apple from the grocery store or a French fry from McDonald's, you've sampled the fruits of the Columbia water.

Today, Washington and Oregon are known more for high-tech than tall timber or irrigated fields. Airplane maker Boeing is one of the largest employers in the Northwest, rivaled only by the likes of Microsoft and perhaps Starbucks. Along the way, the Native Americans, as they did in every other part of the country, paid a heavy price for this progress. In recent years, more progressive thinking has sought to help redress some of those costs, although the battles still are being fought. The salmon, too, paid a heavy price for the development of the river. They are now benefiting from more attention as people recognize that there is as much value in providing water for fish as for farmers.

The Columbia continues to churn out power to the people of the Northwest and supply water to farmers who feed the hungry. The river still enters the Pacific Ocean with enough power and might to send a trail of fresh riverwater 200 miles out to sea. The Columbia is still the heart and soul of the Northwest. President Harry Truman once said that World War II never could have been won without the dams of the Columbia River. Certainly, the West could never have been won without the Great River of the West.

16 MILLION–6 MILLION B.C. The Columbia Plateau is created from lava flowing from the Rocky Mountains.

13,000–10,000 B.C. The Bretz Floods carve channels and coulees into Columbia Plateau, now part of eastern Washington and Oregon.

c. 12,000 B.C. The first confirmed evidence of humans inhabiting Columbia River area appears.

c. A.D. 1500 Rumors start about a Northwest Passage across the New World.

1792 Captain Robert Gray, an American, enters the mouth of the Columbia.

1805–6 Lewis and Clark and the Corps of Discovery reach the Pacific Ocean and winter at Fort Clatsop.

1810–11 John Jacob Astor sends expeditions to compete with British for the Northwest fur trade.

16 million–6 million B.C.
The Columbia Plateau is created from lava flowing from Rocky Mountains.

13,000–10,000 B.C.
The Bretz Floods carve channels and coulees into Columbia Plateau, now part of eastern Washington and Oregon.

1792
Captain Robert Gray, an American, enters mouth of the Columbia.

1824
Hudson's Bay Company moves its operations from Astoria to Fort Vancouver.

1834
Reverend Jason Lee establishes a Methodist mission in the upper Willamette Valley.

16 million B.C.   1750   1800

c. 12,000 B.C.
The first confirmed evidence of humans inhabiting Columbia River area appears.

1805–6
Lewis and Clark and the Corps of Discovery reach the Pacific Ocean and winter at Fort Clatsop.

1810–11
John Jacob Astor sends expeditions to compete with British for the Northwest fur trade.

1848
Oregon becomes a U.S. territory.

1847
The Whitmans and others at the mission are massacred.

1843
Dr. Marcus Whitman returns with 900 American settlers in the Great Migration.

1811   David Thompson of Canada's Northwest Company traverses the Columbia from source to mouth.

1818   The United States and Britain agree to place the border at the 49th parallel, from Minnesota to the Rocky Mountains, and provide for joint occupation and settlement of the Oregon Territory.

1821   Hudson's Bay Company merges with the Northwest Fur Company.

1824   The Hudson's Bay Company moves operations from Astoria to Fort Vancouver.

1831   Nez Percé and Flathead Indians travel to St. Louis asking for the "white man's book," ushering in era of missionary interest in the Northwest.

1832   Captain Benjamin L.E. Bonneville heads west with wagons and traverses Rockies over South Pass.

1933
The Rock Island Dam is completed, the first dam on the Columbia.

1942
Grand Coulee Dam is completed, forming Roosevelt Lake and drowning Kettle Falls.

1992
Lonesome Larry is found in Idaho. The American Rivers Council cites Columbia as the most endangered river in America.

1855
Isaac Stevens signs treaty with Indians creating three reservations.

1918
Billy Clapp is interviewed in Wenatchee World about his idea for a dam at Grand Coulee.

1945
Atomic bombs are dropped on Japan and the real purpose of Hanford site is revealed.

1850

1950

2001

1860
The Oregon Steam Navigation Company is organized.

1883
The Northern Pacific Railroad is completed from Minneapolis to Portland.

1885
The Canadian Pacific Railway connects Montreal with Vancouver, British Columbia.

1938
The Bonneville Dam is completed.

1982
David Sohappy and others are arrested in the "Salmonscam" operation for illegally selling salmon.

2001
Two million salmon are counted at Bonneville Dam, the most since the dam was completed in 1937.

1980s
Columbia Gorge is discovered as a top windsurfing site. The Columbia River Gorge National Scenic Area is created in 1987.

1834 Nathaniel J. Wyeth begins construction of Fort Hall on the Snake River to aid the fur trade business; it is later sold to Hudson's Bay Company and becomes a stopping-off point on Oregon Trail. Reverend Jason Lee establishes Methodist mission in the upper Willamette Valley.

1836 Dr. Marcus Whitman and Henry Spalding arrive in Oregon with their wives, the first white women to go over South Pass. The Hudson's Bay Company steamboat *Beaver* runs between Fort Vancouver and Pacific Ocean.

1841 The first true wagon train heads west along the Oregon Trail with two fur trappers as guides, and twentysome settlers arrive in Oregon.

1843 Dr. Marcus Whitman returns with 900 American settlers in the Great Migration. The constitutional convention on the Willamette takes place.

1846 The Oregon Treaty is signed, extending the United States–Canada border along the 49th parallel.

1847 The Whitmans and others at the mission are massacred.

1848 Oregon becomes a U.S. territory.

1849 The California Gold Rush begins.

1850 Fort Dalles is established on the Columbia, near the Methodist mission, to help emigrants on the Oregon Trail. The first American steamship arrives on the Columbia River.

1853 Washington becomes a U.S. territory.

1854 Gold is found near Fort Colville, Washington.

1855 Isaac Stevens signs a treaty with Indians creating three reservations.

1855–59	The Indian Wars break out.
1859	Oregon becomes a state.
1860	The Oregon Steam Navigation Company is organized.
1870s	Nez Percé War
1883	The Northern Pacific Railroad from Minneapolis to Portland is completed.
1885	The Canadian Pacific Railway is completed, connecting Montreal with Vancouver, British Columbia.
1889	Washington becomes a state. A canal is built temporarily connecting the Columbia with the Kootenay River at Canal Flats in Canada.
1893	The Great Northern Railroad is completed from Duluth, Minnesota, to Seattle.
1918	Billy Clapp is interviewed in *Wenatchee World* about his idea for a dam at Grand Coulee.
1933	Rock Island Dam is completed, the first dam on the Columbia. President Roosevelt authorizes building the Grand Coulee and Bonneville dams on the Columbia.
1937	President Roosevelt visits Grand Coulee Dam. A bill authorizing Bonneville Power Authority (BPA) is passed by Congress.
1938	The Bonneville Dam is completed.
1941	Woody Guthrie spends a month touring the Columbia and writing songs for BPA.
1942	Grand Coulee Dam is completed, forming Roosevelt Lake and drowning Kettle Falls.
1945	Atomic bombs are dropped on Japan and the real purpose of Hanford site is revealed.

1960   The Dalles Dam is completed, covering Celilo Falls.

1968   David Sohappy is first arrested for illegal fishing.

1969   Judge Robert Belloni rules that native fishing rights supersede state law.

1982   David Sohappy and others are arrested in the "Salmonscam" operation for illegally selling salmon.

1980s   Columbia Gorge is discovered as top windsurfing site. The Columbia River Gorge National Scenic Area is created in 1987.

1992   Lonesome Larry is found in Idaho. The American Rivers Council cites the Columbia as the most endangered river in America.

1994   Spending to save the Columbia River salmon is estimated at $350 million per year.

2001   Two million salmon are counted at Bonneville Dam, the most since the dam was completed in 1937.

CHAPTER 1: Promise of a River

1. Quoted in Timothy Egan, *The Good Rain: Across Time and Terrain in the Pacific Northwest* (New York: Alfred A. Knopf, 1990), 15.
2. John Eliot Allen, Marjorie Burns, and Samuel C. Sargent, *Cataclysms on the Columbia: A Layman's Guide to the Features Produced by the Catastrophic Bretz Floods in the Pacific Northwest* (Portland, OR: Timber Press, 1986), 88.

CHAPTER 2: Search for a Secret Passage

3. Quoted in Egan, *The Good Rain*, 27.
4. Quoted in Stewart H. Holbrook, *The Columbia*, The Rivers of America series (New York: Rinehart & Co., 1956), 31.
5. Quoted in William Dietrich, *Northwest Passage: The Great Columbia River* (New York: Simon & Schuster, 1995), 56
6. Quoted in Holbrook, *The Columbia*, 27.
7. William Denison Lyman, *The Columbia River: Its History, Its Myths, Its Scenery, Its Commerce* (New York: G. P. Putnam's Sons, 1909), 37.
8. Quoted in Holbrook, *The Columbia*, 33.
9. Quoted in Ted Morgan, *A Shovel of Stars: The Making of the American West 1800 to the Present* (New York: Simon & Schuster, 1995), 21.
10. Quoted in Gerald S. Snyder, *In the Footsteps of Lewis & Clark* (Washington, DC: National Geographic Society, 1970), 16; in Lyman, *The Columbia River*, 71; and in Dietrich, *Northwest Passage*, 77.
11. Quoted in Lyman, *The Columbia River*, 76.
12. Quoted in Stephen E. Ambrose, *Undaunted Courage* (New York: Simon & Schuster, 1996), 266.
13. Quoted in Robin Cody, *Voyage of a Summer Sun: Canoeing the Columbia River* (New York: Alfred A. Knopf, 1995), 214.
14. Quoted in Morgan, *A Shovel of Stars*, 30; and in Murray Morgan, *The Columbia: Powerhouse of the West* (Seattle, WA: Superior Publishing Company, 1949), 49.

CHAPTER 3: Early Settlement

15. Quoted in Lyman, *The Columbia River*, 122.
16. Quoted in Dietrich, *Northwest Passage*, 231.
17. Quoted in Morgan, *A Shovel of Stars*, 139.

CHAPTER 4: The Americans Are Coming

18. Jeanette Eaton, *Narcissa Whitman: Pioneer of Oregon* (New York: Harcourt, Brace, 1941), 156.
19. Quoted in Robert Clark, *River of the West: Stories from the Columbia* (San Francisco: HarperCollins, 1995), 115.
20. Quoted in JoAnn Roe, *The Columbia River: A Historical Travel Guide* (Golden, CO: Fulcrum Publishing, 1992), 132.
21. Quoted in Clark, *River of the West*, 162.
22. Ibid., 165.

CHAPTER 5: Development of the River

23. Quoted in Holbrook, *The Columbia*, 93.
24. Lyman, *The Columbia River*, 256.
25. Quoted in Holbrook, *The Columbia*, 226.
26. Ibid., 228.

CHAPTER 6: Dam It Up

27. Quoted in Roe, *The Columbia River*, 97.
28. Quoted in Clark, *River of the West*, 261.
29. Ibid., 268.
30. Quoted in Dietrich, *Northwest Passage*, 303; and in Blaine Harden, *A River Lost: The Life and Death of the Columbia* (New York: W. W. Norton, 1996), 82.

CHAPTER 7: The Promise Fulfilled.

31. Quoted in Harden, Blaine, *A River Lost: The Life and Death of the Columbia* (New York: W. W. Norton, 1996), 151.

BIBLIOGRAPHY

Allen, John Eliot, Marjorie Burns, and Samuel C. Sargent. *Cataclysms on the Columbia: A Layman's Guide to the Features Produced by the Catastrophic Bretz Floods in the Pacific Northwest.* Portland, OR: Timber Press, 1986.

Ambrose, Stephen E. *Undaunted Courage.* New York: Simon & Schuster, 1996.

Clark, Robert. *River of the West: Stories from the Columbia.* San Francisco: HarperCollins, 1995.

Cody, Robin. *Voyage of a Summer Sun: Canoeing the Columbia River.* New York: Alfred A. Knopf, 1995.

Dietrich, William. *Northwest Passage: The Great Columbia River.* New York: Simon & Schuster, 1995.

Eaton, Jeanette. *Narcissa Whitman: Pioneer of Oregon.* New York: Harcourt, Brace, 1941.

Egan, Timothy. *The Good Rain: Across Time and Terrain in the Pacific Northwest.* New York: Alfred A. Knopf, 1990.

Freeman, Lewis R. *Down the Columbia.* New York: Dodd, Mead and Co., 1921.

Goetzmann, William H. *Exploration and Empire.* New York: Knopf, 1966.

Harden, Blaine. *A River Lost: The Life and Death of the Columbia.* New York: W.W. Norton, 1996.

Hawgood, John A. *America's Western Frontiers: The Story of the Explorers and Settlers Who Opened Up the Trans-Mississippi West.* New York: Knopf, 1967.

Hill, William E. *The Oregon Trail: Yesterday and Today.* Caldwell, Idaho: Caxton Printers, 1987.

Hine, Robert V., and John Mack Faracher. *The American West: A New Interpretive History.* New Haven, CT: Yale University Press, 2000.

Holbrook, Stewart H. *The Columbia,* The Rivers of America series. New York: Rinehart & Co., 1956.

Holbrook, Stewart H. *James J. Hill: A Great Life in Brief.* New York: Knopf, 1955.

Lyman, William Denison. *The Columbia River: Its History, Its Myths, Its Scenery, Its Commerce.* New York: G. P. Putnam's Sons, 1909.

Martin, Albro. *James J. Hill & the Opening of the Northwest.* New York: Oxford University Press, 1976.

Matsen, Bradford. *Northwest Coast: Essays and Images from the Columbia River to the Cook Inlet.* San Diego, CA: Thunder Bay Press, 1991.

Morgan, Murray. *The Columbia: Powerhouse of the West.* Seattle, WA: Superior Publishing Company, 1949.

Morgan, Ted. *A Shovel of Stars: The Making of the American West 1800 to the Present.* New York: Simon & Schuster, 1995.

Netboy, Anthony. *The Columbia River Salmon and Steelhead Trout: Their Fight for Survival.* Seattle, WA: University of Washington Press, 1980.

Newman, Peter C. *Caesars of the Wilderness: The Story of the Hudson's Bay Company.* New York: Viking, 1987.

O'Neil, Paul. *The Rivermen.* New York: Time-Life Books, 1975.

Parkman, Francis. *The Oregon Trail.* Garden City, NY: Garden City Publishers, 1959.

Roe, JoAnn. *The Columbia River: A Historical Travel Guide.* Golden, CO: Fulcrum Publishing, 1992.

Snyder, Gerald S. *In the Footsteps of Lewis & Clark.* Washington, D.C.: National Geographic Society, 1970.

Wheeler, Keith. *The Railroaders.* New York: Time-Life Books, 1973.

Williams, Richard L. *The Loggers.* New York: Time-Life Books, 1976.

WEBSITES

Astoria-Warrenton Area Chamber of Commerce. Official Site for
Astoria and Warrenton, Oregon.
http://oldoregon.com

Discovering Lewis & Clark. Home page.
http://lewis-clark.org

Center for Columbia River History. Columbia Basin Resources.
http://ccrh.org/ center/resources.html

End of the Oregon Trail Interpretive Center. Home page.
http://endoftheoregontrail.org

Grand Coulee Dam Area Chamber of Commerce. Home page.
http:// grandcouleedam.org

Lewis and Clark Trail. Home page.
http://lewisandclarktrail.com

Maryhill Museum of Art. Home page.
http://maryhillmuseum.org

National Park Service. Fort Clatsop National Memorial.
http://nps.gov/focl/

National Park Service. Lewis & Clark National Historic Trail.
http://nps.gov/lecl/

National Park Service. Whitman Mission National Historic Site.
http://nps.gov/whmi/index.htm

Oregon State Parks.
http://oregonstateparks.org

Public Broadcasting Stations. The Journey of the Corps of Discovery: A
film by Ken Burns.
http://pbs.org/lewisandclark/

Wasco County Historical Museum. Columbia Gorge Discovery Center.
http:// gorgediscovery.org

Who2. Who2 Profile: D.B. Cooper.
http://who2.com/dbcooper.html

Washington State Parks and Recreation Commission.
Washington State Parks.
http://www.parks.wa.gov

The Dalles.
http://www.el.com/to/the/dalles

D.B. Cooper.
http://super70s.com/Super70s/News/1971/November/
24-DB_Cooper.asp

Grand Coulee Dam.
http://www.owt.com/users/chubbard/gcdam/

Department of Agriculture Forest Service. Columbia River Gorge.
http://www.fs.fed.us/r6/columbia

Bonneville Power Administration.
http://www.bpa.gov

Bonneville Dam.
http://www2.Kenyon.edu/projects/dams/bonne.html

FURTHER READING

Ambrose, Stephen E. *Undaunted Courage.* New York: Simon & Schuster, 1996.

Cody, Robin. *Voyage of a Summer Sun: Canoeing the Columbia River.* New York: Alfred A. Knopf, 1995.

Dietrich, William. *Northwest Passage: The Great Columbia River.* New York: Simon & Schuster, 1995.

Eaton, Jeanette. *Narcissa Whitman: Pioneer of Oregon.* New York: Harcourt, Brace, 1941.

Egan, Timothy. *The Good Rain: Across Time and Terrain in the Pacific Northwest.* New York: Alfred A. Knopf, 1990.

Harden, Blaine. *A River Lost: The Life and Death of the Columbia.* New York: W.W. Norton, 1996.

Holbrook, Stewart H. *The Columbia,* The Rivers of America series. New York: Rinehart & Co., 1956.

Morgan, Ted. *A Shovel of Stars: The Making of the American West 1800 to the Present.* New York: Simon & Schuster, 1995.

page:

4: © James A. Sugar/CORBIS

18: © Hulton|Archive by Getty Images, Inc.

25: © Hulton|Archive by Getty Images, Inc.

30: © Hulton|Archive by Getty Images, Inc.

34: © Hulton|Archive by Getty Images, Inc.

36: © Joel W. Rogers/CORBIS

44: Courtesy Library of Congress,
LC-USZC4-2115

49: © Hulton|Archive by Getty Images, Inc.

51: © Hulton|Archive by Getty Images, Inc.

57: © Michael Maslan Historic Photographs/
CORBIS

68: © Underwood-Underwood/CORBIS

78: © Joel W. Rogers/CORBIS

Frontis: Federal Caucus, Bonneville Power Administration (BPA), SalmonRecovery.gov
Cover: © Michael T. Sedam/CORBIS

ABOUT THE CONTRIBUTORS

TOM LASHNITS is a writer and editor who specializes in history, culture, and the economy. He worked as a researcher and writer at Time-Life Books, where he was assigned to The Old West series, and served as an editor at *Reader's Digest* magazine, where he edited a series on great American rivers, among many other features.

TIM MCNEESE is an Associate Professor of History at York College in Nebraska. Professor McNeese earned an Associate of Arts degree from York College, a Bachelor of Arts degree in history and political science from Harding University, and a Master of Arts degree in history from Southwest Missouri State University. He is currently in his 27th year of teaching.

Professor McNeese's writing career has earned him a citation in the "Something About the Author" reference work. He is the author of more than fifty books and educational materials on everything from Egyptian pyramids to American Indians. He is married to Beverly McNeese, who teaches English at York College.